I0539666

Erotic Tranquility II

The Languid Effect

A Steamy Trails Anthology

Erotic Tranquility II - The Languid Effect

Cover design by Katrina Gurl
Book design by Katrina Gurl

Printed in the United States of America

Steamy Trails Publishing:
www.steamytrailspublishing.com

ISBN-13: 978-0692331286
ISBN-10: 069233128X

Dedication

Couples are always forgetting to lust for one another with immersible passion. This book is dedicated to the art of making passionate love, releasing all inhibitions.

Languid means: Drooping or flagging from weakness or fatigue; faint.

Allow sex like this to happen to you every once and a while and become OVERWHELMED with satisfying sex!

Acknowledgements

We, of Steamy Trails Publishing would like to thank all the writers that toiled to seduce us yet again.

Contents

Introduction

The first, Amazon bestselling STP anthology, "Erotic Tranquility: Eroticizing the Masses" was a literary success. "Erotic Tranquility II" brings you more passionate, sexy, and original stories written by writers you know and love. In "The Languid Effect," the stories again sets the stage for seduction, stimulating, playful and romantic tales. If you are addicted to sexy fiction, then this is the book for you!

My Secret Love Affair
by Keeta B.

"Dammit, Jamie!" I shouted. Why can't I seem to get this man out of my head? Jamie was this fine looking brotha who lived down the block from her. He was the most attractive being she had ever laid eyes on. This man stood six foot eight inches tall and had all the masculinity in the world. He has dark short hair, dark mocha skin, smooth, juicy, kissable lips and perfectly straight white teeth. When Jamie would take his shirt off to work on his car all you could see were the outlines of rips and dips of pure muscle. He was as lean as the best cut of meat at the butcher shop. All I knew was he needed to be mine.

I'm Jasmine Mayweather. I live on 108th Avenue and Lennox Blvd in a quiet brownstone apartment. Just recently, I graduated from NYC with a degree in Communications. Currently I'm working part-time at Radio Shack, while looking for a full time gig with a radio station or broadcasting company. I'm 23 years old, no children and no significant other as of yet. Since I've moved to this neighborhood I've had the pleasure of meeting this handsome guy named Jamie Brownlee. One day I was walking from the corner store listening to music through my head phones when I damn near ran him over. I wasn't paying attention and the music had me feeling some type of way. I was grooving and moving in all sorts of ways and didn't pay much attention to the person standing on the sidewalk.

Before I knew it, I was falling all over this man. "Excuse me, I didn't mean to run you over like that." I'm Jasmine Mayweather and I live down the block in those two-toned brownstones. "Oh, you're all right, I saw you were pre-occupied and didn't notice me." Jamie said with a smirk on his face. I'm Jamie Brownlee, and as you can see this is where I reside. Hypnotize! I couldn't say anything else because his beauty had me mesmerized to the point I couldn't talk. I was beyond stunned. This man had it going on!

It seemed like every day after that little incident I looked for Jamie whenever I went out. Always hoping I would have the opportunity to bump into him once again. His scent was forever entrapped in my skin. The aroma of Usher cologne was to die for. His hormones and the scent of the cologne were a great combination. It made me feel tingly inside and out. I had a "Jones" for this guy. When I went to sleep at night I would dream about this man and couldn't get his face out of my head. The way he touched me body the day I damn near plowed over him sent electricity throughout my body causing it to tingle all over. From the sight of this man he had my pussy doing a dance and pulsating at a rate it had never done before. Thinking of the things I would do to him was making me hot and heated. I'm no virgin...that man could truly get the business any day of the week.

I must be crazy to even think that man noticed me. He was only being polite because of how we met, but to have truly noticed me like I did him was a far cry from reality. Nah, he didn't notice me. I'm not they eye grabbing kind of girl. When I look in the mirror all I see is a girl with perfectly flawless medium brown skin, two dimples in each cheek, deep light brown eyes that are deeply set, and short bob-styled hair. I consider myself an "average" looking individual. I'm not a show – stopper like I'm sure he's used to.

To test my hypothesis I began making trips to the corner store a little more frequent than I normally would. There would be times I didn't even need anything from there but would make it seem like I had to go just so I could see Jamie. His scent filled the still air and seemed to make its way into every inch of my nose. When I would get a whiff it made it seem as if I was floating on air. On my way back from one of my many trips to the corner store I felt a pair of eyes homing in on me. As usual I had my headphones on and the music was bumping. On this particular day I was wearing a tight fitting pair of Levi jeans, a half shirt with my school logo on it, and my Space Jam colored Jordan's to match. This time as I was walking, I made sure I kept my ears open and began to look around. Just when I was about to make my way past Jamie's brownstone apartment I spotted someone sitting on the stoup. It was him. He was looking ever so handsome. He had a fresh haircut, had grown his goat-tee out just a little and was wearing some True Religion jeans and matching shirt. As I walked by it appeared his eyes were following me. He wore this devilish grin on his face and was showing those beautiful white teeth. I had to find the nerves to get at this guy. I spoke and he returned the favor. No other words were spoken, but if only he knew how I was feeling about him at that moment, there wouldn't be any need for words only action.

Several days later I was coming out of my apartment to catch the bus for work I noticed Jamie was at the bottom of the steps.

"Hi, what brings you to my humble abode?" I asked.

Jamie looking all around as if he didn't realize I was talking to him. "Oh, I was just in the neighborhood and decided to stop by and see if you wanted to go grab a bite to eat." Jamie replied. I began to giggle.

"In the neighborhood? Really Jamie? Are you for real? You only live down the block you're always in the neighborhood." I responded back in my cutest school girl voice.

Jamie responded back, "Girl, you know I was being sarcastic, but on the real, I do want to have a bite to eat with you."

"I like your style and would love to spend a little time with you to get to know you better."

I damn near pasted out. Those few words took my breath away. 'Oh my fucking God this man just asked me out and I've been beating my head in trying to find a way to get this man to notice me." The Lord sure does know how to answer prayers.

I looked at my watch and noticed I only had approximately five minutes before the bus would run and I had about a fifteen minute walk. "Fuck, fuck, fuck!" "What's wrong?" Jamie asked?

"I just realized what time it was, I'm going to be late for work and the bus I normally catch will be here in about five minutes and I have a fifteen minute walk to catch it before it pulls off." Jamie showing those pearly whites said,

"Well how about I give you a lift? That way we can stop and grab a bite to eat?"

"That would be awesome, let me finish locking up and we can go."

We walked down the block to where Jamie lived. His car was parked on the curbside as usual. He drove a hunter green 1978 Camaro. He had stock rims on it and a bra on the front. This car was a classic. He unlocked the car door and then opened it up for me and I proceeded to get in. He then walked around to the driver's side and got in. We pulled off and headed to this quiet little barbeque joint three blocks away. Monroe's BBQ joint was the best place to get your grub on this side of town. The coleslaw was to die for and the way the pulled pork melted in your mouth gave food an entirely new meaning. While I was in college all my classmates talked about was Monroe's. I grew up in Newark and had never tasted anything like this before; so all my friends got together and brought me some back to the dorm. I was in pure heaven by time I finished eating. Ever since then, this has been my secret place to run off to when I'm not feeling my best.

Since I no longer had to catch the bus we decided we had enough time for us to sit down and eat rather than do a take-out order. We laughed and talked for what seemed to be hours. I learned more about Jamie than I ever expected to know. He told me he was 29 years old, had a younger sister named Nina who was a nail tech, he works as a mechanic at a local dealership, has a little 2 year old son named Javier, and had been to prison for 18 months on a simple battery charge. Jamie also told me he has never been married, and his birthday is August 10. He bragged about how good Leo's are and how I should make it my purpose to get to know one. The entire time he talked he showed off those pretty teeth. I asked him what made him go to prison because I don't view him as the violent type. Jamie responded, "This bitch ass boy decided to put his hands on my sister Nina. That was a wrong move for him so I had to beat his ass to show him who he was fucking with. I will kill for those I love and hold dear to me." I couldn't do anything but respect him for his honesty. If it was me I would do the same exact thing.

It was now my turn to tell Jamie about me. I told him I was 23 years old and had just graduated from NYC with my Bachelors of Science in Communication. I am an only child and my parents live in Newark where I grew up. I currently work at Radio Shack downtown and was looking for a gig with a local radio or broadcasting station. I am currently single, a home body and my birthday is February 14. I am the type of person who believes in love but I don't go out looking for it I feel if it's real then it would find me. Before I could say another word Jamie asked me if I found him attractive. In my mind, I'm saying: "what does he mean do I? Hell yeah I do!" Next thing I know, he leaned in and gave me the wettest kiss I have ever had in my life. It was breathe taking and intense, full of passion. When he finally released my lips from his front teeth I had to shake my head and regain my composure. He then spoke, "So what happened to your last boyfriend may I ask?" Blah, blah, blah was the only thing I could muster up and say. He started to laugh. "That's okay; grab your stuff so I can get you to work. We have plenty of time for you to answer my questions."

On the drive downtown I finally found words to answer the questions Jamie asked of me. I was glowing inside and out and knew I had found a lover in him. As we pulled up to my job he reached over and grabbed my chin and planted yet another kiss on my lips. He then handed me a sheet of paper with his cell phone number written on it. "Don't worry about catching the bus home tonight, call me and I'll be to pick you up." Said, Jamie. I wrote down my number on a napkin I had in my pocket and handed it to him. Then I got out the car and nodded my head in agreement to what he had just said. I was giggly on the inside and had a smile as big as the sun on my face. His actions answered all the questions I had been asking myself since I first bumped into him weeks ago. He not only found "me" attractive, but he wanted to spend time with 'me, a nobody' and it made my heart gleam with joy.

I called Jamie on both of my breaks and we talked and laughed like we had known each other for years. I informed him that I was in charge of closing the store tonight and had to do inventory afterwards and told him I hoped it wasn't too late for him to pick me up. As I had already told my other two co-workers they could go home early and I would take care of the store.

Normally one of them would stay and walk with me to the bus stop to make sure I was safe. They repeatedly asked if I was sure and I confirmed to them "yes." I'm sure; I have someone coming to pick me up. I knew this would draw their suspicions of who this mystery person could possibly be. I love the two I work with on a regular but they are some nosey people.

Towards the close of business the store got real busy for some strange reason. I sold more items within the last 20 minutes of the store being open than I had all day. Maybe this was a sign things were looking up for me. I could only hope at this point. Ten thirty rolled around and Jamie was pulling up in front of the store. He watched me as I locked up the store and he got out of the car, walked around to the passenger side and opened up the door for me. Once I was in comfortably he closed the door then walked back around to the driver's side and we pulled off.

"How was your night?" asked Jamie.

"It was good. I got a little busy towards the end of my shift, but overall it was a decent night." Jamie then asked if I was hungry and wanted to stop and get a bite to eat. I told him I was okay and just wanted to get home and take a hot shower then curl up under my blanket then watch a movie. Jamie mumbled under his

breathe, "Wish I could take a hot shower with you."
That put a bigger smile on my face. I pretended I didn't
hear him and stared straight ahead the remainder of
the drive to my place. When he pulled up he parked the
car and turned it ignition off. He then turned his body
so he could look directly at me and said, "I know you
heard what I said and I'm waiting on an answer. Can I
come up and join you in that hot shower you're about
to take?" This man is unbelievable. My instincts are
saying no it's too soon to have this man in your place,
but my body was saying, you better tell him yeah before
he finds someone else to take a shower with. I quickly
nodded my head yes and got out the car.

Jamie followed me as quickly as he could. I opened the
door to my apartment and left the door wide open for
him. He came in stripping all of his clothes off showing
that chiseled body I love so much. I was trying to get to
the bathroom to turn on the shower, but Jamie stopped
me by grabbing my arm and spinning me around,
planting a deep, long, passionate kiss on my lips. His
tongue was so far down my throat I had trouble
swallowing. I felt my knees giving from up under my
body and he quickly caught me and picked me up and
carried me into the bathroom shutting the door behind
us. He turned me around placing my back against the
door and began undressing me with his teeth. My
pussy was quickly heating up I couldn't resist this man's
touch. In no time Jamie had me standing butt ass naked
in the bathroom and he stood back to admire my body.
"Um hmm delightful and succulent." He exhaled. He

planted his juicy wet lips on the tip of my nipples making his way around my entire areola.

The passion he used when he sucked my breast had my body feeling tingly and weak. I needed for him to stop so I could compose myself but I also needed this man at this very moment. While he was sucking on my breast with one hand he undid the button on his jeans and had them wrapped around his ankles in record time. He released my breasts from his lips and stood back. I couldn't help but to admire the girth of this man's penis. It was so large and thick. I couldn't believe he was packing a fucking 10 inch long 6 inch wide dick in them jeans. Who would have ever thought he had all that going on. Don't know how I'm going to take all of that but I guarantee you once I get it I'm going to keep on getting this dick. My head was spinning a hundred miles an hour, but I knew I was about to partake in an adventurous ride of a lifetime.

I could feel the steam from the shower causing the temperature in the bathroom to rise. The mirrors began to cloud up and so was my body core. I'm more than positive if someone was to take my temperature at this very moment it would read well over 105 degrees. My pussy was swelling up and juices were beginning to flow. Jamie must have been reading my mind. He guided me into the shower and washed, caressed, touch, pinched and kissed every inch of my body. It was tantalizing and hypnotic. I was falling so hard for this guy. I know I need to reevaluate this situation and not rush anything but I was hooked from the first time I laid eyes on him. Here he is in my bathroom taking me on a fantastic ride like no other man has ever done. It felt wonderful.

We made love in the shower, on the floor, standing and when it finally had gotten too heated in the bathroom we made our way to my king sized bed and used up every inch of it. This man had given me more orgasms than I have ever experienced in my entire time having sex. He knew exactly what he was doing and how I was responding moaning and groaning, arching my back and sweating like a Hebrew slave. There was nothing I could do or say at this moment. I was spent.

After hours of love making, we fell asleep holding each other. The last thing I remember was Jamie kissing me on my forehead telling me how he had a great time and wanted to see me on a more regular basis. I told him that would be great and drifted off to sleep. When I woke the next morning Jamie was gone. He left his shirt with a note attached to it.

"Sorry I had to leave so soon, work calls. I'll be by later to finish what we started last night. Here are a few dollars for you to get a bite to eat and catch the bus to work." - Jamie.

I unfolded the bills and counted them, $100.00. Wow! No one had ever left me that kind of money before. Boy do I feel special. I looked at the time on the clock it read 6:45 a.m. I decided to roll back over and get a few more minutes of sleep. When I woke back up, it the clock read 8:15 a.m. I'd better rush now I have to be at work in 2 hours and need to grab a bite to eat. I forced myself to make my way into the bathroom, turned on the shower. The aroma of sex still filled the air in the shower area. We most definitely did some things while in here. Giggling. While the shower was heating up I decided to explore my closet to find something to wear to work. I decided on a red see through blouse and black slacks. Found my name tag in my purse and adhered all items I found necessary for the day. Several minutes later I headed back into the bathroom and took a long overdue shower. Flashbacks from the night before filled my head and placed a smile on my face. Who would have thought he would notice someone like "me."

Oh well, can't worry about that, the point is he did and just didn't care. I could feel myself smiling the entire walk to the bus hub and then again the entire time I rode the bus. It's going to be very obvious when I walk into work what happened to me, but I really didn't care at this point. I couldn't hide the smile that was entrancing my face. I had gotten the man I dreamed of and wanted for some time now. I don't care if the entire world finds out. I've been alone for way too long and it my time to have someone in it if only for a short time. Jamie was the oldest man I have ever dated and for him to take interest in me was an accomplishment.

When I arrived at work I was wearing the same Kool aid grin I had been all morning. My two favorite co-workers had already opened the store and were assisting a few customers. Walking in I said, "Hello" to everyone and proceeded to the back to put my items in the back storage room. As I was walking I overheard Jessie telling Craig about this abusive ex-boyfriend. I kept walking as if I didn't hear what they were talking about. As I was hanging up my jacket, the first person to come in the back was my home girl, Jessie.

"So, Miss Thang what's with this Chester Cheetah grin you wearing?"

"I don't know what you're talking about Jessie. It's a beautiful day outside and I'm enjoying being alive, that's all."

"Oh, come on Jas you ain't fooling anyone it's written all over your face. It must be that new mystery man who's been picking you up."

"Maybe it is maybe it ain't either way it's my business and until I'm ready to speak on it, we'll just leave it where it's at." I replied. Jessie storms out of the back room with tear stained face.

"What's her problem?" I asked Craig. "She's just upset Jas, somehow her abusive ex-boyfriend found out where she lives and works. She scared for her life." Responded, Craig. I never knew Jessie had an abusive ex. We've all hung out together after work but she's never mentioned she was abused by her ex-boyfriend. I feel so bad for her. I'm going to give her the rest of the day off and let her compose herself. I'll go by her house on my lunch break and check on her. She has me worried.

Every few minutes I would look at the clock to check the time. Jessie was on my mind and I couldn't shake it. When it was time for my lunch break I walked the four blocks to where Jessie stayed. I banged on the door and she wouldn't answer. I became even more worried...what if this man had come and done something horrible to her? Maybe I should have inquired what it was she and Craig were talking about when I first walked in, but I was too caught up trying to enjoy my own moment that I didn't ask.

I walked back to Radio Shack and told Craig about Jessie not being home when I arrived. He didn't look surprised at all. Wondering what could have happened I questioned Craig. "Did you know she wouldn't answer the door and you knew I was going over to check on her?" Silence filled the room. Craig had his head bowed down and he slowly raised it up. "Jas, you just don't understand what all Jessie has been through."

"You're right I don't, but I want to understand." I shouted in a brusque tone. Once again Craig looked me in the eyes and said, "Jessie saw you with your new lover/boyfriend the other night when he came to pick you up."

I do not understand what he means. "What difference does it make if Jessie saw me with my date?"

Craig with the look of disbelief on his face cried out, "Because it's her abusive ex you were with!!!"

Storming out of the store with tears streaming down my face, I couldn't believe what my ears just heard. How could this be? Jamie doesn't seem like the type of person to harm a fly. I had to get to the bottom of this. I pulled my cell phone out and called Jamie and told him to meet me at the corner of Saks 5th and Montgomery.

Standing by the corner pacing I spotted the green Camaro from a block away. Jamie pulled up and opened the door from the inside and I got in. He then leaned in as if to give me a kiss and I quickly pulled away.

"What's wrong beautiful, I was worried when you called?" Asked Jamie.

"Just drive, Jamie we will talk once we get to my place!"

We drove in silence and I contemplated the questions in my head that I wanted to ask him. Minutes later we pulled up at my brownstone. I got out of the car and slammed the door and ran up the stairs to my place. Jamie ran full speed up the stairs after me. When he entered the apartment I was balled up on the couch in a fetal position crying my eyes out. Not knowing what to do Jamie held me and asked why I was so upset. My nose running and sniffling I found the voice to tell him the information I was given. Jamie was appalled. He looked me in the eyes and kissed my face and said, "Baby, it's not me. I swear to you I have never in my life seen or known this woman. She has to be mistaken." Jamie came even closer to me and began undressing me. He kissed me from the top of my head to the soles of my feet. He made love to me in a way I was yet prepared for. It was mind blowing and invigorating. Unfortunately, that wasn't enough, I was still confused and didn't know what to believe. After we finished an intense love session, I turned to Jamie and told him I need for him to come to my job so Jasmine could make a positive identification and prove him wrong. I couldn't continue seeing this man if he is a liar and abusive to his women.

Jamie agreed and several days later he met me at my job. I had him come around 3p.m. since I knew Jas would be getting off at 4. He walked into the store and Jas was the first person to spot him. She froze up and began yelling. "Get the fuck outta here! How dare you come to my place of employment to try to intimidate me? You fucking bastard."

I ran from the back to see what was going on and grabbed Jas to calm her. "Jas what's wrong this here is my friend Jamie and I told him about the mix up and he came to prove to you he doesn't know you."

"So that's what he's calling himself? That bitch name is not no damn Jamie its Javier and he lives on Maryland Drive and Oyster St." yelled Jas.

"Now hold the fuck up young lady! I've never laid eyes on you before until this very moment. You have me mixed up with someone else and whoever it is, it ain't me." Jamie egregiously responded. "And, for the record, I've never lived in that neighborhood you claim I do. Just ask your girl where I live, she will vouch for me."

Everyone stood looking stunned. Jas walked over to me and grabbed me at my collar on my shirt. "You have got to believe me. I wouldn't lie about something like this." Torn I didn't have any words to speak or the knowledge to know the truth. What I did know was we had to get to the bottom of this. I couldn't have my

friend and co-worker scared to death like this. In mid
thought Jasmine's phone rung. She looked at the name
on the caller ID and then showed me. "It's him, what do
I do?" I've got to think fast. "Answer the phone, put it
on speaker and act normal." Jessie answered the
phone and the caller began yelling obscenities. Jessie
was so nervous she hung the phone up. Next thing we
know a man came barging into the store and we all
froze. Jamie was looking just as stunned as we were.
We were seeing double. How could this be? Twins?

Jamie rushed the guy and asked him who the hell he
was and how in the hell did he look just like him. As far
as Jamie knew he only had a sister, but this fool was a
splitting image of him. Jessie ran off leaving us all to
deal with this cat. Craig had unknowingly to us called
the police and they soon barged in the store a few
minutes later. We soon discovered the man's name
was James and he was given away at birth. James had
been the one who dated Jessie and was the abusive
boyfriend she had been talking about and not my Jamie.
I was pleased to find that information out.

The police arrested James and took him down to the
station. Come to find out, several other women had
filed complaints about him and he was a wanted man.
We were all ecstatic to find out the news and to have
this criminal off the streets. Jamie was sad and wanted
some answers also. Craig called one of the other stores
and asked them if they would send someone over to
help run the store. He then told me to take the
remainder of the day off, go find Jessie and give her the
good news and be supportive of my man. I took that

advice and did just that. Craig handed me my jacket from the back room and I grabbed Jamie's hand and we left.

Once in the car, I asked Jamie if he was going to be okay. He assured me he would be. I was doubtful so I leaned in and planted a kiss on his cheek and told him I was there for him. He smiled showing those beautiful teeth I love to see, and we pulled off. Jamie drove to the outer part of the city and didn't speak a word. I could tell his mind was racing a thousand mile an hour so I let him have his peace. Soon we pulled up at this set of duplexes and parked. Jamie got out the car and walked over to my side and opened the door. He held my hand to assist me in getting out of the car. Once out, he planted a deep passionate kiss on my lips and told me this was where his mother lived and he needed for her to give him some answers. Shaking my head up and down I knew this visit wasn't to say hi and keep it moving. These visit maybe his last if he didn't hear the answers he wanted to hear.

Before we could even knock on the door, it swung flying open. There at the door stood a petite woman of 5'1 inches tall with her hair covered with a bonnet. Jamie didn't say a word and pushed his way pass her. Jamie went in the living room and sat on the couch. He waited for her to come in before he started in on her. By the look on her face she knew what this visit was about. "I'm sorry baby; I didn't want you to find out about your brother like this." I was only a teenage girl when I got pregnant with you and turning tricks to get by. I gave up your brother so he could have a good home and a family to love him." She cried.

"Cut the bullshit mama. You could have told me long before now I was a twin. You see the shit he's out here doing to women. I could never do something like that. I could have gone back to prison for this type of shit. You got my girl all concerned and not trusting me. What kind of mess is that? How could you do this to me?" Jamie sobbed with crocodile tears in his eyes.

I jumped up from the chair I was sitting in and wrapped my arms around him as tight as I could. "It's okay baby, I'm here for you. When you ready to go just nod your head and we can leave." Jamie then nodded his head and we left.

We drove back to my place. Jamie was distraught by the news he received from his mom. Pondering what I could do to console him I did the only thing I knew to do. I undressed Jamie and kiss his body all over. When I got down to his pants I rubbed my lips over his zipper where his penis sat. I slowly undid the zipper and reached inside his pants and pulled out his thick penis. Using both hands I began to massage it. Wetting up my lips I slowly place them on the tip of his penis and lowered my mouth all over it. I began to suck and slob on it slowly. He must have been enjoying himself because he passionately grabbed the back of my head to assist with the motion. Faster and faster, deeper and deeper I took that dick in my mouth. When he had enough he pulled me up and placed me on the floor next to where we stood. He spread my legs open and removed my panties. He opened up the lips to my pussy and began to lick sending chills up and down my body. I loved what he was doing to me. He climbed on top of me and forced his dick into my pussy and it instantly began to flow my precious juices. I was whipped and this man meant the world to me. I can't believe I didn't give him the benefit of the doubt before not trusting him. This love making session would surely make up for all the doubt. We made love until the sun came up the next day.

Early the next morning my phone rang and it was Jessie calling to apologize for the mix-up. I told her anyone could have done the same. She wished me the best with my relationship with Jamie and I thanked her for her support. I wasn't feeling my best and ran to the bathroom. Jamie rushed in behind me to see if I was alright. I told him I had missed my period this month. He looked at me with sparkles in his eyes. "I'm going to be a daddy!" he yelled. Then he got down on one knee and pulled this small black box from behind his back. He then took my hand and looked me dead in the eyes and proceeded to ask, "Miss Jasmine Mayweather would you do me the honor of being my wife?" Tears flowing from my face I answered, "Yes!"

Six months from the time of this entire ordeal I had gotten my man and found out I was having his baby. Jamie no longer went to visit his mom, but he told her about the baby. Jessie no longer worked at the store and moved to D.C. with her parents, and life was good. Jamie was waiting on me hand and foot and our love making sessions never seemed to get old. I knew from the first time I laid eyes on this man I was in love. For all this to come true is only a blessing from God.

About Keeta B.

Keeta B. is a pseudonym being used by Nakita K. Borders. Nakita grew up in Battle Creek, Michigan and graduated from Battle Creek Central High School. After being there the majority of her young adult life she moved to Arkansas with her 4 children. Once settled she moved to Pine Bluff, AR where she studied Nursing and Sociology at the University of Arkansas Pine Bluff, before moving her family to Fort Worth, Texas where she currently resides. Once moving to Texas she began her studies at the University of Texas, Arlington where she will be receiving her bachelor's degree in University Studies with her emphasis in Social Science, Human Science and Humanities. Nakita will graduate in December 2014.

Keeta B. began writing while attending high school and she always had a love for reading books. Over the years, Keeta B. felt a sense that everyone has a story to tell and it all starts by putting it on paper. She hopes that this book encourages and possibly inspires others to live their dream of getting their stories out. Her first novel, "Life's Memories" is available on Amazon and wherever book are sold.

A DICK SO DAMN GOOD
by Brooklen Borne

Jordon and I have been good friends since our first lunch date. We would talk almost every day, either by phone or in person, for hours. I was feeling him sexually but I had him wait; six months before I gave him some of this yum-yum. I had to make sure he was worthy of enjoying my sexy as body. It was a wait, well worth it for the both of us.

I remember that day, as if it was yesterday. Oh, how I remember that day. It was an unusual cool and gloomy fall afternoon. I called him and told him, that I wanted to stop by and show him something. He said he was doing some transcribing and I could come by anytime. An hour later I was knocking on his apartment door. He opened the door and greeted me with a smile and firm hug. He smelled so good, I gave him a spontaneous soft kiss on his neck.

"Let me take your coat." He said with a serious expression. I just stood there for a second, in my black three quarter length London Fog trench coat and black red bottom stilettos. Then I slowly undid my belt and unbutton my coat. When I opened my coat to reveal nothing underneath but a see through red bra and matching panties, the expression on his face was priceless; not to mention that massive imprint I noticed that instantly formed in his jeans.

He got on his knees, not taking his eyes off mine and placed both hands on my right thigh. The blade of his hand brushed against my pussy and my clit came from behind the hood, to see what was going on. His soft but masculine hands, slowly traveled down my legs, until they reached my ankles; slipping of my shoe. He repeated the act to the left leg. My pussy was so wet, I think I had a mild orgasm. He then placed his thumbs along my panty waistband and lowered them. As soon as I stepped out my sexy under garment, his tongue flickered my clit. "Oh shit!" I blurted out as, my legs buckled and I came in his mouth. He took ahold of my left leg and placed it over his shoulder, as I leaned back against the wall. I held onto his head, biting down on my bottom lip; as he ate me out with precision. My pussy was so wet and the slurping sound he was making, had me losing my damn mind. I was on the verge of climaxing again, when he suddenly stop and slowly stood up. He assisted me in removing my coat and bra; dropping both articles to the floor.

"Go to the bedroom." He commanded, and like a good soldier I followed his orders. I glanced back and his eyes were affixed on my ass. I smiled, as I turned back around and got in his plush and cozy bed. He didn't immediately followed me into the bedroom. I was wondering, what was his hold-up, then I heard music playing. He had put in a cd by KEM, before entering the room. Taking off his shirt, I wanted to touch his chiseled torso but when he took off his jeans, and I saw that rock hard dick, my pussy began twerking.

He reached out for my hand, getting me off the bed and turning me around. My thighs pressed against the side of the bed he softly pressed against my back; positing me in a ninety degree angle; with a pillow under my head. He told me to grab my ass cheeks and separate them. Just before I felt his mouth and tongue make contact with anything it wanted to back there, I moaned softly; gathering up the sheet in both my hands. I came twice in a matter of minutes. He slapped and massaged my ass; for a few seconds before putting the dick to me. His rock-hard dick became the invisible man as it disappeared deep into me. My soft moans turned into grunts and screams of passion as he held onto my hips and fucked me unmerciful. The music of KEM might have filled the air, but it played back-up to my vocals; as I talked in tongues.

"Evonne, you feel so damn good."

"Oh daddy, you do too! Ahhh, ahhh, oh God!" I screamed out, as he thrust rhythmically inside me. I lost count on how many times I came, as I was becoming light headed. Shit, this man dick is lethal I thought to myself as I had an orgasm, that made me a certified freak. He pulled out and got on the bed and instructed me to get on top; so I can ride him. He became my drug and addiction. I wasn't planning on getting hooked on Jordon, but it was too late. I was his, to fuck any way he pleased. An orgasm was building up in me, like no other I have felt with any other man. I was riding his shit, as if I was doing a pony express route. He held onto my hips, with occasional squeezed of my breast; as we fucked each other stupid. I screamed out his name as my eyes rolled up in my head. I had an orgasm that made me do the Matrix. I opened my eyes and I saw two of everything. I got nervous because none of my past sexual experiences had this type of effect on me. I had lost track of time, how many times I came, and the number of positions Jordon had me in; as he fucked the shit out of me.

Our animalistic sexual behavior was in full effect as I groaned, moaned, cussed adjectives out loudly and enjoyed the out-of-body fuck of my life. I was on the verge of not being coherent as positioned me, to hit the pussy doggy style. The music of KEM, was no longer playing; but the sound of the bed squeaking, my screaming and pleading, took over number one; on the Bill Board Chart. Jordon held onto my hips and power drove that good dick in and out of me; that my mind, body, and I believe my soul, was no longer mine; but his. I could feel myself losing consciousness as he continued to fuck me like a convict; just released from prison.

My moans and screams of passion slowly became silent. The grip of my grasp on his sheets was no longer strong. I couldn't believe what was happening to me. A euphoric feeling consumed me as I slowly began to enter a dream-like state. I could feel Jordon still fucking me; with that good dick. A dick so damn good, that I passed out.

About Brooklen Borne

Brooklen Borne is a native New Yorker who grew up in the Brownsville section of Brooklyn. He began writing short stories in his sophomore year of high school, based on his street experience. His high school English teacher enjoyed his stories and advised him that he should enter his writings in the state wide writing contest. He didn't follow through with her suggestion because the streets were more appealing.

Upon graduating from High School, he enlisted in the Marine Corps. During his tenure, Brooklen had a chance to visit and live in some of the most exotic places in the world, meeting interesting people along the way. This life experience inspired him to write again, incorporating some of these character's in a few of his stories.

Brooklen has completed four novellas, two novels, and a book of short stories. His work has been promoted through blog talk radio shows, book signings and other literary events.

He holds an Associate's Degree from Charminade University in Honolulu, Hawaii and a Bachelor's Degree from National University in La Jolla, California; both are in Criminal Justice with a minor in Behavioral Science. Brooklen currently resides in the United States.

Tasty
by Anthony Arnold

Staring at your body after we make love

I trace the sweat that runs between your breasts

The look in your eyes

Silently asking for more

I long to taste your body

I kiss my way down your body

Licking every curve

Savoring every part of you

Finding your flower I want to make it bloom

I kiss, caress, lick and nibble it

Your legs tighten and pull me in closer

Deeper and deeper I go

Tangy and sweet, you are to me

Your scent arouses me

I hear you moaning

As your hands pull me in.

You start to shake as you erupt

I break away and slowly enter as you cum

Your breath catches as you slip over the edge

And you tighten around me

I taste you again as I drink all of you

As you give me all of you

Tangy and sweet

Tasty

The Tub
by Anthony Arnold

Present time

She lay in the tub, her body sated, and still throbbing. She could still feel him inside her. His fullness inside of her. She reached out to him but no one was there. She closed her eyes and remembered...

Earlier that evening...

She waited for him in the kitchen. Dinner was almost ready and she was standing. Waiting. The door closed and a smile came to her face. Her man was home.

She turned to see him and her breath caught. He had a look about him that she had never seen before. A dangerous look. She knew then that this night would be unlike any other.

He walked toward her and swept everything off of the table. She ripped his shirt away and began to kiss him all over his chest. He ripped away her dress to expose her petite body to him. He was a big man and all ways, and she had never been able to take all of him.

He raised her to his mouth and she gasped as he took her with his tongue. She cried out as he tongue lashed her to the point of passing out. The orgasm hit unexpectedly, and she did something she had never done before. She squirted into his mouth as she passed out.

She went to her knees in front of him, ripping his pants off as she went down. She heard him groan as she tried to suck his soul out through his dick. He took her head in his hands as he slid in and out of her mouth. She stared into his eyes as he fucked her face.

He pulled away from her and placed her on the table and slid into her wetness. She screamed as he plunged into her. He legs automatically went to his shoulders as she knew that was what he liked. She could not take it all, but she took what she could.

In her mind she knew that this was different. Something that she had not experienced before. This was not the lovemaking that she knew. This was something different. This was fucking!

He picked her up and held her in his arms as he leaned against the wall. Her arms wrapped around his head and her legs around his waist. No sounds were heard except those of their bodies slapping together and their moans. She came again and dug her nails into his neck.

They continued to fuck all over the house. He did her doggy in front of the fireplace. She rode him in the den. They spooned on the back porch, and on the hood of the car in the rain. Each time she came as if her life depended on it.

He carried her to the bathroom and placed her into the tub. Warm water engulfed her as she settled inside. A small orgasm escaped her as her body settled in. as he turned to leave, she knew then what she must do.

Baby. Don't leave. Take me here. Right here in this tub. I want to take all of you. Right here. Right now. He looked into her eyes as he tried to grasp what she was saying to her. Give it to me. I want all of it inside me.

He got inside of the tub and kissed her. A soul stirring kiss that made her wet, even though she was in a tub of water, made her feel different. Slowly he started to slide within her. She felt the familiar feeling of being stretched and feeling full. She came as he entered her. He was the only one who had ever been able to do that to her. As he got to the point of no return, he looked into her eyes as if to ask, are you sure? She never wavered. In a trembling voice she said, give me all of you.

Slowly he gave her what she wanted, what she craved, what she had dreamed about. He pushed in until he was in to the hilt. She cried out as she felt him bury himself inside her. Fuck me she said as he gave her his dick. Fuck me with that big cock, yes fuck me. Her orgasm came back to back. Not knowing where one stopped and the other began. A sound escaped her lips, like that that of a wild animal. But she didn't care. She had to have it.

Finally he couldn't hold out any longer, and buried himself deep inside and flooded her womb. She screamed and everything went black.

Present time...

Laying in the tub, her body was still excited. She could still feel his fullness inside of her. She brushed her fingers against her clit, and felt a small orgasm escape her.

He walked in unclothed, with a tray of food for her. She stared upon his impressive manhood, smiled and thought. I know what's for desert!

~~ FINIS? ~~

Self-Love
by Anthony Arnold

She gazes upon herself in the mirror. Not bad she thinks. Breasts firm, flat stomach, and a tight ass. Her hands flow over her body. Her breasts begin to ache, her nipples rising. She feels that familiar longing in the pit of her stomach. Her body craves release. It craves satisfaction.

Slowly walking to her bed, she thinks about her lover. Her passion starts to flow as she thinks about him ravishing her. But no, not tonight.

Tonight is all about her.

Lying on her bed, she lets her mind take control. She imagines his touch as he slowly kisses his way along her body. Her breath quickens as she feels his lips caress her breasts. She sighs and shakes as she feels his tongue tracing the route to her forbidden fruit.

Her hands tease her body as her imagination runs wild. She feels the object of her desire as it rises from its hiding place begging to be touched. Her fingers slowly caress it, covering it with her love juices. She imagines his lips fastening themselves around it as he flicks it with his tongue. Her body shakes with her first orgasm as she rubs slowly. Gently.

Her juices flow into a puddle on the bed, but she doesn't care. Her body is covered with sweat. Her moans echo in the silence of the room. There is nothing but her.

And him.

She feels herself heading to the point of no return. She pulls her legs up and slides a finger deep inside her wetness. She gasps as her vagina grasps it. She imagines him entering her, deeply slowly. Her body shakes with each thrust. She cries out as she brings herself time and time to the edge, only to let herself fall away.

Finally her body betrays her. Orgasm after orgasm ravishes her. No! No! She cries out but she is too far gone. Her body shakes until she is spent.

There is nothing but the sound of her shallow breathing. A single tear runs down her face. A small smile and maybe a telephone call.

Maybe.

~~ FINIS? ~~

4 words
by Anthony Arnold

As I stared into the most beautiful brown eyes I had ever seen

An ebony goddess said 4 words that would change my life forever

Do you trust me?

As I started to speak, she silenced me with a kiss, a deep soul stirring kiss then she started to undress me, all the while kissing, and biting here and there until I was naked and again she said,

Do you trust me?

She kissed me again, and slid a black hood over my head. Slightly frightened, but strangely aroused I let her lead me to an X-shaped brace where I was strapped in. I felt her graze me with a leather quirt, as she began to trace my body and all parts of me when all of a sudden I felt pain like I had never known up and down my spine. I cried out, but the beating became much more intense, but then after a while, I began to crave the pain it became exquisite, I became aroused to the point I thought I would burst.

When she stopped, I begged and pleaded with her not to. I craved release when as suddenly as it began the whipping ceased. She grabbed my erection and began to squeeze as I began to moan, I felt her warm mouth engulf me. I begged her to stop, the pleasure behind the pain was too much to bear, but she wouldn't. I felt my soul being pulled from my body from my dick.

As she squeezed my balls I came with a flood so intense I would have fallen to my knees if I could...as I hung there spent, I heard her whisper those 4 damnable words in my ear,

Do you trust me?

As I was unstrapped and fell to my knees, she ripped the hood from my face there in front of me was the most beautiful pussy I had ever seen nicely trimmed. Clit extended, and wet as the deepest ocean as I stared upon this work of art, I barely heard what she said to me.

Service me!

I dived into her like it was my last meal, I licked, and nibbled and sucked somewhere I heard her say stop, but I would not, I could not. She screamed as she came and sunk to her knees in front of me and I heard those 4 words again. But not what I expected.

Why wouldn't you stop?

I couldn't stop, I wanted you to feel what I felt. She reached in between us and found my growing erection and pushed me to my back and took me with one brutal plunge. She rode me as if her life depended on it. She had to regain control, but her body betrayed her. She began to find herself in the throes of orgasm. I grabbed her hips and slammed myself into her

NO, NO, NO! YES YES YES! She screamed as her pussy began to spasm she began to milk me as I rammed my dick into her harder and harder FFFFFFUUUUUUCCCCCKKKKK MMMMEEEEEEE! She screamed, as she began to cum I pulled her hips down on me and sprayed the inside of her womb with my seed as she fell upon my chest

As we both lay on the floor spent and satisfied fading into oblivion

I swore I heard these words again...

Do you trust me?

About Anthony Arnold

Anthony Arnold, born and raised by his grandmother in a little town called Quincy in Florida, as an avid reader of all genres of literature, Anthony has found a particular passion for black history.

Writing gives Anthony the ability to educate those that have no clue about the things that African Americans have faced and write of things that they will never be taught in schools, such as "African 113 Americans" and the Civil War and shedding light on the strength of our people.

His desire to show the younger generation to want to learn about where they come from and to let them know we are much more than what society has labeled us!

THE VISIT
by Shane Davenport and Carlton J.

Blaise was about an hour drive from Charis. Their long distant love made it hard for them to be with each other throughout the week and busy schedules. Plus, Blaise worked every other Saturday. However, this Saturday was going to be a little different. Charis wanted to see him bad and she had no intentions of waiting for him to get off work. In her mind two weeks was way too long without him.

She arrived at his office and realized that there was hardly anyone there. In her mind this was perfect for what she had in store. Charis wanted to be a little naughty and the few scattered workers that were there seemed to be perfectly minding their own business.

She entered the building and noticed there was no one at the front desk to buzz her in, so she called Blaise's cell. Riiiing...

"Hey baby." Blaise says, as soon as he picks up. "How are you? I was just thinking about your sexy azz...miss the hell out of you, girl!"

"Well, I'm glad you miss me, because I have a surprise for you...go check out at the front desk."

"Go check the front desk? Please don't say you sent flowers again...the guys are still giving me a hard time about that last bundle you sent." He laughs as he walks from his office hastily to see what's at that front desk.

Blaise slides his security card, opens the door and immediately, Charis runs and jumps in his arms! Blaise is grinning from ear to ear, so happy to see her.

"Are you working hard or hardly working?" Charis says with a big grin on her face as well, as she still embraces him. They held on for dear life to one another just a few seconds longer, because two weeks felt like an eternity.

"Today is a little slow...I'm almost finished with that big project, so you couldn't have come at a better time. "He says, hugging and kissing her again.

"Is anyone in your office?"

"Nope. Just me today; all the non-workaholics actually took off for the weekend." He laughs.

"Well can we head to your office; I want to show you something."

"Sure, c'mon." Blaise led her to his office.

"You sure no one will come in here?" She asked.

"Yes, babe...I'll even lock the door if that'll make you feel better. What you gotta show me?"

"This." Charis began to unbutton her blue Eddie Bauer, O neck coat, revealing a black bra and tiny black panties with a red bow in front. Blaise leaned back on the desk to get a full view of her. He was beyond excited, aroused and as hard as brick.

She walked over, placing the coat on the chair nearby, dressed in her underclothes and black heels. Charis kisses his neck and then his lips and begins to unbutton his well pressed white office shirt. As she kissed him intensely she began to undo his jeans. She wanted to feel his hard cock, so she began jerking him off. At first slowly, but faster and faster the wetter he became. Before she knew it she squatted down to taste him. It was so warm, tasted so good and the harder he got the more she wanted suck him.

Charis could tell he was about to cum right in her mouth, but that didn't stop her...she kept sucking his dick and he loved every stroke. Blaise felt the sensation of a nut beginning, but he stopped cumming to plunge deep inside of her.

Blaise knew Charis would continue sucking his dick as long as he would let her but he couldn't wait to see the vibrations of her ass as he stuck his mostly swollen dick. Blaise wanted his dick deep in her pussy to get it rock hard again.

He told her in a demanding way "turn your ass around!" His dick slipped out her mouth as she swallowed drops of him as he pulled away. He fingered her thong to the side of her pussy lips and put his dick right at her opening and pressed it inside of her. She shivered at his firm thrust, but she was dripping wet, so it popped right in.

From behind with a hand full of her ass, in and out, slowly he pressed, until they became unison in rhythm. Blaise had always fantasied about sexting her at work this way, but never did he for once believe it would come true. Blaise love making love to her, but right now, since it had been so long since he'd saw her; he just wanted to fuck. Blaise wanted to let go of all the sex depravation he was feeling.

Blaise was taking long hard stroke deep inside of her and she couldn't tell what kind of stroke he was going to throw on her next. Her hands kept flexing, trying to grip on to the side of the desk; all she could do is hold on to anything in that office that would keep her in rhythm with him. She could tell his passion was jailed for 2 week, because that dick was hitting her strong.

Charis was weakening with every stroke Blaise forced upon her. She must have had at least 4 orgasms...and Blaise must have been on his second wind, because he showed no sign of cumming.

He loved hearing her silent moans and her sudden outburst. He was enjoying the look of her ass slapping against the base of his dick while he held hands full of her ample ass.

Blaise, as if he could read her mind, yanked his dick out of her and turned her around to face him and then he picked her up and made her lay on the desk. He then spread her legs as far as they could go and pulled her g-sting off. He reached up to kiss her lips, then neck and pulled her bra over her breast and licked her firm nipples with his wet, hot tongue.

Blaise kept slowly kissing his way down to her pussy. As he kissed her belly, he stuck two fingers into her wet pussy and licked it off his own fingers, but that was not enough. He wanted to taste her.

She looked at him as he traveled closer to her clit. He tongued her from the entrance to the tip of her clitoris. As Blaise flicked his tongue back and forth across it all she could do is lie back on the desk letting out a breathy moan. He then pushed his tongue deep...going in and out and round and round. He stroked the hood of her clitoris as he slid his middle finger deep, slowly inside of her. After several minutes of fingering her, he gently sucked the clitoris. She moaned louder. Blaise didn't care if his office walls were thick enough to contain her voice. He was enjoying pleasuring her this way.

Charis whispered a moan, as she tried to catch her breath. She grabbed his head as she felt herself about to come, but Blaise just kept right on licking and sucking her clit. He knew she was about to explode and her moans turned him on even more. Her pussy lips were engorged from the play of his tongue. "Baby, what are you doing to me? And, then with a muffled voice, "Baby I'm comiiiing ...Ooooh, Ah, Ooooh ..."

Charis came in his mouth as he kept licking, flicking and sucking her pussy...he seemed to gobble up all of her wetness greedily. Charis couldn't take it anymore and let out a loud gasp in ecstasy "Fuck!"...was all she could say. Blaise continued to let his tongue slide down to her ass.

He followed the juices down to her ass with his tongue slowly. He then pressed his thumb softly against her clit as her body still trembled. Blaise could tell that the climax had drained beyond belief. He then pulled his face away from her pussy and stuck his hard dick inside of her; thrusting deep and hard. Her post climax moaning became screams as he moved his penis in and out of her hot moist tender vagina until he came too.

With a face still full of her cum slathered from under his nose down to his chin he slowly backed away and pulled up his pants. Charis looked at the time and took in a deep breath and (almost) in a drunkard stagger got up to ready herself to leave the office. Blaise wiped his face adjusted his collar and then, bent over to give Charis a kiss as she re-buttoned her coat.

"Mmmm, I taste good on your lips."

"Yes you do and you are going to taste even better tonight! I know you still have the key, so go to my apartment, get comfortable and wait for me to get home." Blaise kissed her again and she could tell he had a much freakier session planned for her later.

About Shane Davenport and Carlton J.

Shane Davenport and Carlton J. have co-authored love stories together many times over as well as dually blogged together for the past six years.

Shane is an online award-winning author of several books and community projects and Carlton is a science engineer, born and raised in Germany.

They were college friends since 1984, meeting at UCLA, both majoring in science. After several years of successful careers, they reunited at a wine tasting in southern California and as luck had it, they both had writing blogs and they turned out to be as compatible as lovers as romance writing buddies. Neither of them believes in marriage, but they have a happy friendship and they two write everyday together, happily.

Another Life, Now
by Victoria Velato

- 1 -

"You know," he said with some gravity in his voice; they'd been working together long enough that she'd learned to tell when he was going to lay something deeper than vacant discussion about current news or sports on her. But then, their daily conversations always got past the niceties and

went straight for the jugular. She liked that about him, but didn't realize how much, until he continued by saying, "In another life, we'd likely be lovers.

"Something stirred deep within her, reacting—despite her reluctance—in the bottom of her heart and with the sudden swelling of her clitoris. It was as if those words turned the key to activate an otherwise-dormant machine. Her engine rumbled to life, partially protesting being awakened after so long. "What do you mean by that, Harry?"

"I mean, if we'd met under different circumstances...if we had proximity on our side, we would probably be more than just creative partners."

"Hmm," she pondered aloud, bottling up the slight offense she felt. Harold was gregarious and always tended to say what he thought. He had no hidden agendas, so his honesty was something she usually enjoyed - until now. His confession was to the point, but that sharp tip punctured something. How the hell did he think she was supposed to respond?

His observation was accurate though: the situation was not to their favor and there were too many miles between to consider anything serious between them. They talked every day. Those discussions were quite revelatory and many things were said in confidence. Though the focus was always book business, there was a strong undercurrent of admiration, bordering on desire. Harry, with all his blatant double-entendres and hilarious comments, never hid the fact that he wanted her.

Paloma protested internally, but her body had made other plans. Her nipples gained sensitivity against the suddenly realized prison of her bra and hardened in defiance.

"How long is it from me to you," she blurted, not thinking of the words before they betrayed her position and escaped lips that wanted to be kissed. Something put in that way usually garnered a bawdy comment from him, but he either missed or ignored the opportunity.

"A few hours," he hummed. "About ten, I think."

"How's that car of yours holding up?"

"You mean the old battering ram," he chuckled. "With the recent repairs, it could handle a road trip."

She was amazed that, with all the money their writing venture was raking in, he insisted on keeping his antique piece of Detroit muscle as his primary mode of transportation. That was something that, as his business partner and friend, she would have to continue to dissuade. But Harry was something of a cheapskate, which also made him a purist of sorts. Though there was plenty of green stuff in his account from their creative output, he wrote for more than just money. His passion toward scribbling was a turn-on.

"Good. What are you doing this coming weekend?" Ever the editor, she analyzed her words and thought how she could've put a spin on them to ask if he wanted to be coming all weekend. But she wasn't so brash—that would've been something he would've said, then half-apologized, inciting laughter on both ends of the phone.

Lack of proximity might not be such a bad thing, she thought. That could keep us from getting hooked and making the typical pitfalls of mixing business with pleasure.

"So, what's the plan," he asked with something she'd never heard in his voice: a smidgen of trepidation. Paloma could hear his thoughts: Am I being invited up to do chores or to have fun?

A bit of both, she thought as she playfully envisioned him unclogging her pipes and sweeping out her caboose.

"The plan, Mr. Palmer,"—she only called him by his last name when they were talking about the business side of their agreement, which put him as writer and her as editor—"is that, because you're such a workaholic, you could use a bit of downtime. Today is Thursday. I authorize and encourage you to set sail tonight and enjoy a long weekend with Yours Truly."

"But we've got a manuscript due to the publisher by the end of the month," he griped, as much the workhorse as he was the joker in the deck of cards. Truly an artist, his ongoing affair with his invisible muse kept books on shelves and the checks rolling it, so Paloma had respect for his indomitable ethic to get the job done. However, she had to admit that she was a bit jealous of the supposedly imaginary being that presented him with seemingly endless series of characters and storylines. Looking at the muse's visitations as those of a mistress, Paloma wanted to give her creative co-conspirator a much-needed getaway.

"We'll make some headway on that," she promised with an intended pun, then paused before saying, "but I have some work for us to do before we get to that."

Harry wasn't used to being checked at his own game. He prided himself with dominating the figurative chessboard of his life. Classic narcissistic control freak— and she was attracted to that about him more than she wanted to admit. Something in her vaginal walls wanted to make him surrender that control for a while and just enjoy himself. She wanted to see the dumbfounded look on the face on the reluctant ladies-man-cum-lone-wolf who'd posited himself as the epitome of cool.

He grinned on the other end of the line, seeing the setup of the board for what it was. Paloma's knight and rook were putting pressure on his king to move.

However, her queen loomed in the shadows, across the black and white spaces, waiting to pounce. There was a reason why the queen was the strongest piece, with her ability to roam about as she pretty much damn well pleased within the kingdom. The philosophy, which most people couldn't get, made perfect sense to him.

Like a mouse sniffing out the cheese displayed temptingly in the trap, he asked, "So, what hotel do you recommend?"

Her voice, which was already deeper than that of the average woman, went down to a husky, suggestive octave. In fact, she purred more than spoke: "We recommend the Paloma Arms"—and hands and thighs and lips and breasts, her mind wandered—"where you will be thoroughly accommodated."

He chuckled playfully, "That's no hotel I've ever heard of."

"That's because," she said, remaining in character, "we don't advertise and only host the most exclusive clientele."

Just then his penis, which had already jumped to life at the probability of seeing her in the flesh, became thick and engorged. He placed his hand on it and squeezed, as if that would make the swelling go down. That only made it worse.

It was hard to make the great, outspoken, bestselling novelist find himself at a loss of words. She smiled at the concept of being able to pull the rug from under him. Her queen moved in for the killing stroke. "Shall we call this a checkmate," she asked.

To that, Harry, who'd taken the silent moment to break out a duffel and begin tossing clothes in it, could only say, "Indeed. Well done, Ms. James."

With all the secrets they shared and getting-to-know-you conversations they had, there was one thing Harry had yet to learn about Paloma that he would discover that weekend: she didn't believe in bemoaning the what-ifs. She didn't buy into having regrets for not taking the road less traveled. More than that, she didn't subscribe to lamenting things that could have been. He plotted out his life meticulously, while she tended to be more daring and spontaneous. In that way, they were perfect for one another: her yin comfortably fitting to the curvature and length his yang. That idea got her nipples hard and found her fingers circumventing her panties to find the soft place between her ample thighs.

Harry mentioned that, in another life, there was a possibility that they could be lovers. Paloma wanted to explore that other life.

Now.

The weekend was here and so was Harry. He arrived in the early afternoon on Friday. A broad shouldered with a warm smile and a mischievous twinkle in his eye, he greeted her with a back-breaking embrace. He held her a longer than necessary, but Paloma didn't mind a bit. She enjoyed the feel of their bodies pressed against each other. She imagined his arms holding her after making love. She took a breath to keep a sigh from escaping.. Harry loosened his hold on her, but held her hand.

"Turn around and let me get a good look at you, girl!" He raised her arm and twirled her around slowly, taking in every womanly curve. "Yaass, yaass," he drawled, "you is a grown woman!" He punctuated the statement with a hearty laugh.

"Well, this grown woman has prepared a wonderful meal for the weary traveller. Hungry?"

"Starving."

Something in the tone of his voice sent heat directly to her lady parts as she led him to her apartment.

Harry continued to enjoy the shape of Paloma's frame as he followed her up to her apartment. Although modestly dressed in black yoga pants and a long, fitted t-shirt, her hourglass figure refused to be concealed. He wondered what kind of underwear she had on. Lace? Thong? Did it match her bra? He wanted to grab those hips and pull her against himself so she could feel what she did to him.

The aroma of cooked meat, herbs, and seasonings snapped him out of his fantasy, as they entered the apartment. Though minimally furnished, her place had a warm and welcoming feel to it. Instrumental jazz, piped in through her computer, filled the air along with the scent of food. He followed her towards the back of her apartment to a bedroom that doubled as an office. There were cartoon flowers and butterflies on the walls. He raised an eyebrow and looked from the smiling blossoms to Paloma. She tried not to laugh.

"My five year old niece spends a lot of time with me. This is her room. She said you could use this weekend as long as you clean up after yourself."

"I will make sure I leave the princess' room neat and clean. May I play with her toys, too," he asked with a chuckle.

"No, but if you work hard on this project, I might let you play with a few of mine," Paloma teased.

To that, Harry snickered and gave a coy bow, as if he was the acquiescent knight piece. Seeing her made him want to make all sorts moves in the queen's boudoir. She blushed, bit her lip, and pointed to a door in the hallway. "Bathroom is right here if you want to freshen up. Lunch will be ready soon and then we can get down to business."

She turned and made her way toward the kitchen. He noticed her bare feet and the beaded ankle bracelet she wore. He placed his bags in the closet, washed his hands, and walked into the kitchen. She was standing on her tip-toes stirring a pot of something that smelled wonderful. He stepped behind her, gently holding her hips, sniffing her hair and kissing her temple. She stopped stirring and leaned into him.

"What's for lunch?"

"Beef stew," she said, softly.

"Looks delicious," he said, nipping at her ear and neck and thinking, Yeah, the food would probably taste good, too.

"I'm an excellent cook, but if you keep doing that, the food is going to burn and we'll have to order pizza."

He immediately let her go and stepped back with a wide grin. "On that note, I'm gong to take a nap. Finish cooking that food, woman!"

She laughed, grabbed a towel, and snapped it at him as he made his retreat from the kitchen.

- 3 -

They worked on writing and editing as the meal that was meant to be lunch was enjoyed as an early dinner, then settled in to watch a movie, more concerned with the sensation of their legs touching than the fate of the on-screen characters. They enjoyed the lack of personal space between them. Each tried to devise a subtle means of creating less space without seeming forward. Harry made the first move, turning toward her and gently sliding his hand up her thigh, stopping just shy of what he longed to see and touch and taste.

She didn't stop him. She slid her leg onto his lap, over his growing erection. She took his hand and moved it into position. He bit his lip and began to feel for Paloma's sweet spot through the fabric of her pants. He moved his fingers in a circular motion, as he leaned in and planted soft kisses along her neck. She rotated her hips to match his strokes and he moved his fingers faster.

"That feels so good," she purred.

"You like that, huh?"

Paloma nodded and whimpered softly.

"I'm going take your pants off, ok?"

She nodded, too overcome to speak.

Harry didn't stop kissing her as he reached around and latched his thumbs into the waistband of her yoga pants and slid them down her shapely legs. He saw her red, lace panties and felt his penis struggling to escape its confines. He wanted to slide into her wetness and feel her muscles contract around him with every stroke. But he couldn't rush. He wouldn't. Not with her.

In what seemed like one motion, she removed her t-shirt, straddled his lap and began to massage the noticeable bulge in his jeans. She leaned in, her full breasts just under his chin and kissed his forehead, his cheek, and lips. She lingered there for a moment before taking to nibbling on his ear. All the while, she slowly rubbed her hand over his erection and finally whispered, "You should let him come out to play."

"Coax him," he replied with a teasing smile.

From the stiff knot she felt in his slacks, there was little need for encouragement, but she welcomed him into her world. Harry tried to maintain control and a cool head while his lover anointed the crown of his proud soldier. Beads of perspiration suddenly appeared on his nose and forehead and he lolled sleepily, almost in a trance. He released a whimper and she knew that he was hers.

"Like that?" the snake charmer cooed, allowing his thick-necked cobra to get a bit of air before taking the plunge again. Her mouth engulfed him and he let loose a low, unbroken moan. "Yeah," she said, "I think he's feeling like he's the center of attention."

Her tongue swam up the length. On her way back down, she varied the technique, flicking about the underside, feeling him quake, until she got down to where the wide stump of his tree met scrotal earth. He shuddered, brown knuckles turning figuratively white as he gripped the back and arm of the sofa as she sucked his testicles ever-so-softly. Then she went to licking them like a kitten with a saucer of milk.

"That's it," he seethed, shaking his head back and forth vigorously, as if in denial. In fact, he was on that Egyptian river, fighting the sensation of losing full control and so willingly giving her his seed. But at that point, she could've had anything she wanted from him. He was hers.

"Mmm hmm," she hummed, taking the length until the crown touched the back of her throat.

Harry nearly lost consciousness. His eyes rolled back until the whites showed. He was possessed, though not by any sort of demon, and if she was an unclean spirit, he would gladly take a sentence in the depths of her fiery pit for all eternity.

The intensity hit its apex, clawing and digging into his back, sinking its teeth into his neck. The express elevator from the main lobby of his skyscraper took off like a thunderbolt, zooming toward the penthouse, threatening to blow through the roof. He grit his teeth and growled like a beast. Paloma smirked as much as she could without gagging on how much harder he became as he was about to cum. Harry cursed, the terra cotta color of his face flushing closer to red. He inhaled a deep breath through pursed lips that chilled his teeth. He lifted his pelvis from the seat, forcing the final, angry inch into her voracious mouth. He wanted to empty himself into her throat, for her to drink of him if she desired. Ever the gentleman, he did not grab her head and force her onto his impending geyser. To busy his hands, he made them into fists and began pounding the couch cushions.

She could feel the eruption build and prepare to explode from the cycloptic eye, and she grabbed the base of his penis, staunching his orgasm. He groaned through gritted teeth, went through the symptoms but, like a stifled sniper, he didn't get permission from his spotter to release. He jerked, clinched and fought the undercurrent that wanted so desperately to surface.

"You can't come yet," she purred, smiling.

Eyes wide and dumbfounded, Harry watched as Paloma rose to her feet, doffing the red lace panties and spread herself in one smooth motion. Her pussy was wet, pink and thirsty for a drink.

"This," she said, pointing at, then inserting a finger into the tunnel between her Indian-grapefruit-colored labia, "is where you come."

He stood, his erection pointing the way, magnetized by the sweet cavern framed by her voluptuous thighs.

"And don't worry," she said, "I'm fixed."

Oh, I'll fix you, he thought with a chuckle. With that, he slowly slid his length into the physical manifestation of her invitation. He waited for the moan to escape when his fire helmet hit her back wall, then pulled out suddenly. It was more pain for him than she would realize, but he was trying to make a point for them to both anticipate and enjoy. He was teasing her as much as himself. Resisting the bestial urge to penetrate and ride her, he took in her ample beauty. The girl was thick and pleasant to look at, as well as to touch. She looked up with a bit of a scowl, but it didn't last long. Before she could register complaint, she felt him returning the favor, her vagina becoming the impromptu saucer and her lover, the hungry feline. Taking her swollen clitoris between his lips and sucking with a steady, intense rhythm, her shuddering made Harry grin.

Paloma licked her lips as she watched him taste the contents of her honeypot. Her deep brown eyes were intense, watching his head move up and down as his tongue gained intimate knowledge of her womanhood. He looked up into her eyes, wanting to see her reaction as he dined, and enjoying every sigh, gasp and moan as he made love to her.

- 4 -

The humming of his tenor voice against her clit sent chills to her core. She gasped in pleasure, but he wasn't done. He relaxed his lips and blew gently, causing his lips to vibrate against the very same, stimulated spot. Paloma arched her back and grabbed his head. She moved her hips in a circular motion as he continued to vary between licking and sucking and blowing. Her body began to shiver and quake. She was about to explode and he was prepared to enjoy the sweet taste of her nectar when she pulled away and pushed Harry to the floor. He was taken completely off guard. She straddled him and said, "I'm sorry, I can't wait anymore. I want you, NOW." Then she slid her warm, wet, pussy over his rock hard erection and began to gently rock and rotate her hips. His eyes were closed and he gritted his teeth in a way that looked like he was in pain, but his pleasure was evident in the way he gripped her ass and hips. He didn't want her to stop. He slid his hand over her leg and moved his thumb right over her clit and gently massaged it. She lost her rhythm when he touched her. His touch sent an electric sensation throughout her body and she wanted him to touch everything at once to quell the intensity of her impending orgasm. She wasn't ready. She wanted to enjoy his hardness inside of her just a little longer. He sensed her yearning, and took his time giving her exactly what she desired.

Although Harry was usually the earlier riser between the two, it was Paloma whose eyes opened first. She stared up at the ceiling, studying the detail of the concentric pattern that had been fancifully placed there. Her lover/coworker was wrapped around her in such a way, she never needed covers during the night. Even with the stickiness between them, she had to admit that it felt good. Maybe, too good.

The drive back to Detroit would be the same, arduous ten hours it had been for him to get to her. She knew his story: hit the road early to maximize daylight so he could be home in time for dinner. But there were two things that bothered her about that scenario. Being an editor and spending so much time making suggestions and alterations to the tales he spun, she wanted to offer another ending. She didn't want him to go and, being a bachelor, he would probably wind up eating a microwaved burrito or something else posing as food for his supper. He stirred, as if he could sense her thoughts in his dreams. Harry released a small sigh, then a yawn, the warm exhalation feeling good on her neck.

They had both rocked, shook and held each other, taking one another with the fervor of mating beasts, then enjoying long, languid kisses between romps. Paloma wasn't much for kissing. Oh, she relished the play of lips, the breathing in of air in a tight space. The problem was, kissing was terribly intimate. It had been a long time since she'd simply locked lips and allowed her eyelashes to tickle a lover's face. But Harry, for all his seeming gruffness, was different. She'd kissed him outright...and often. Morning breath aside, she was tempted to wake him up with a smooch that she hoped would turn into a session of speaking in tongues. Her writer had a marvelous way with that pink, long, nimble thing in his mouth. Not only did it make her knees buckle when he put it to her lips, it made her pelvis gyrate when he used it on her lower set.

She was becoming wet again at the thought. Though her plan had been to shuffle him out the door in time for Sunday service, she didn't want him to leave just yet and she wasn't ready to ask forgiveness for their weekend of sin. Not yet - maybe, not ever. Her bed had become a purgatorial place, the hell only being the concept of his departure.

He had filled her with his seed several times since he'd arrived. She could sense those little soldiers swimming about inside, desperately seeking an egg they'd never find. And, in that moment, Paloma found herself doing something dangerous: imagining a life with the children she'd never have, dreaming of Harry hitting the back wall of her cervix as often as the urge struck, and having as many children as her body would allow. He'd author and she'd edit, a metaphor for how their relationship already was. Tears suddenly felt like a thousand little pinpricks, filling her otherwise dry eyes. She lay there in the arms of her weekend lover, reluctantly and quietly weeping for another life they'd never have together.

About Victoria Velato

Victoria Velato made her writing debut in the first edition of Erotic Tranquility in 2012. She discovered the joys of writing sensual poetry and stories shortly after getting married. While remaining quiet on the literary scene since publishing her first short story, she continues to write and explore the writing craft in her free time. Victoria is a licensed massage therapist and yoga instructor living in Philadelphia, Pennsylvania with her dog Coco.

Dionysius Burton, DioBurto Photography

Interludes to Die For
by Pat "Trishvision" Brown

As I was lying across the bed wearing nothing but my panties, I realized that not only was I not interested in the murder mystery that we had planned on watching but I had developed a raging fire inside of me that needed immediate attention. I was sprawled out and slightly twisting, because she was throbbing. I gazed at him with a ravishing desire in my eyes as he sat on the floor leaning up against the bed wearing nothing but his underwear. I scooted towards him and rubbed my face against the side of his face. His goatee was smooth yet slightly rough; just the way I liked it.

I leaned my upper body over the side of the bed and lowered my head down towards his protruding manhood. He looked at me in disbelief, but I was on a mission. I positioned myself on my forearms and released the lollipop I was so anxious to taste. He moaned. I moaned and licked as best I could from my acrobatic position. I eventually got completely on the floor as we continued our impromptu excursion. Needless to say the movie remained a mystery to us.

He and I becoming us started out normally; like any other relationship. Jerry saw me working in a department store. I was the cashier and I guess he thought I was beautiful. Yeah, I guess he did. Anyway, he slipped me his number after making small talk. He didn't ask for mine. In retrospect, I wonder if it was because he was so fine that he thought I couldn't resist giving him a call. I have to admit; he was fine. But I didn't call him, not sure why, but I just didn't. Actually, I didn't even give it much thought, and that was surprising because I am usually a sucker for a pretty face.

Months had gone by and I was hanging out with a friend on the other side of town. As we were walking, I looked over and noticed Jerry standing there in front of an apartment building, speaking with a young lady that was sitting on a bike. I smiled and said hello respectfully. He replied and I kept walking. My friend and I traveled about a block when I noticed the girl jerry was with was riding towards us on her bike. She asked me to come over to the street; that she wanted to ask me something. Thinking she had plans of starting trouble, I refused and continued to stroll with my friend.

About two months later on New Year's Day, I was bored after recovering from a hangover I had acquired from wild partying the night before. I decided to glance through my phone book to see if any interesting names popped out. Of course Jerry's name was calling out to me. When we spoke, he seemed surprised to hear from me considering I had his number for quite a while and never used it. I asked him about the girl on the bike; if she was his woman. He said she was his sister and she just wanted to give me his number again but wasn't sure if the guy I was walking with was my man. We both laughed.

Actually we talked and laughed for quite a while that evening. We offered information about ourselves including the fact that I was five years older than him. I said that was cool as long as we both conduct ourselves as responsible individuals. After all he was at least legal.

We got together a couple of days after that and quickly became intimate. We had an intense magnetic attraction. It was like we had become inseparable. There was something about him that was different from anything I had ever experienced. I believe I was turned on by his adventurous spirit when it came to lovemaking. I mean we had some wild times. We hung out with friends and went out on dates but more often than not, we acted like uncontrollable nymphomaniacs.

Our first intimate encounter took place in a hotel. He picked me up in his truck. Just the way he looked at me made me feel exquisite; like he was completely captivated. As I entered the vehicle he made sure that I buckled up. He referred to me as precious cargo. I smiled as my heart just melted. When we arrived to our destination, he carried everything into the building and up to the room. We had brought food, Alize', baby oil, scented candles, a radio, cd's, and clothes. He also brought work clothes because he had to go to work the next morning.

After we got situated, I showered and laid in the bed naked, still a little shy, I pulled the sheets over my body. I sipped a cocktail while enjoying the smooth sounds playing on the CD player. As soon as he exited the restroom he came to me and proceeded to massage my body. He started at my neck and then loosened the tightness from my shoulders and upper back. Everywhere he rubbed he kissed and/or licked; down my spine to small of my back. The way he manipulated my ass was magical; like a celebrated potter strategically handling his clay. My thighs thanked him. The back of my knees as well as my calves were pleased. He worked his way down to my feet, and I may as well have been floating on air. He then turned me over and did the same on the front side. He was sure to complete the full body massage before detouring to target specific erogenous zones.

After rubbing my feet he came up and gently kissed me on my lips. Then he kissed, licked and fondled every yearning inch of my being, even areas I didn't realize desired attention. There was no half-stepping; this guy meant business. When he entered me, a tear streamed down the side of my face. I came right then and there. But there were many more pleasurable releases that evening. We made unbridled passionate love on a level incomparable to any I had ever experienced. I excreted everything from tension to pleasure to appreciation and gratitude for God answering my prayers of experiencing love the way it was designed to be...Beautiful. Laying there basking in the aftermath, I felt like silk.

We had turned on the turbo as far as being together. We immediately got an apartment together. He seemed to be in more of a hurry than me which I never understood, because everywhere we went women would literally swoon over him. To be honest, I almost felt like a monster while in his presence, at least that's how his admirers looked at me. He definitely had an aura that women were drawn to, but he never disrespected me while they swooned.

Our relationship gave permission to release all my inhibitions. We explored expression anywhere, everywhere; in the car, on the beach, I even did a dance in a lace cat suit for him. I would have never imagined myself doing something like that before meeting him. I had chosen a song by the Whispers called "Give It to me". There was a part in it that I liked that said "Serve it cold, I'll make it hot". I had practiced performing in the mirror whenever he wasn't around. The cat suit I had purchased was crotch-less and a little too tight, so my tits tended to jump out from time to time. Of course that only added to the entertainment.

After I completed my amateur dance, I decide to give him an intimate lap dance. I instructed him to take a seat in a dining room chair that I had brought in the bedroom. I stalkingly approached him and seductively gyrated my curves towards him. His eyes lit up as his joystick stood up. We were both anxious to take it to the next phase.

I positioned myself over him and sat down directly onto his waiting penis. It entered so smoothly, we sighed simultaneously. I pushed my pelvis forward and moaned as my breasts hit his chin. He lowered his head to taste a mouthful. I pounced on him vertically, swerved horizontally and pumped him with fierce circular motions. My legs moved like a leap frog as he grabbed my ass, squeezing it and rolling it around even more. I was wetter than I had ever been. Breathing intensified and sweat poured from our bodies. I exploded three times before he allowed himself to cum. I fell on him like dead weight for a few seconds then fell onto the bed. He showered as I convulsed amidst bliss for a while.

We had many interesting intimate encounters. Often times we were in an alter state of mind though. I mean we usually drank liquor and from time to time we indulged in other spirits such as marijuana, mint leaf and on a couple of occasions PCP.

In hind-sight there were some red flags that I ignored. One time in particular should have been the straw that broke the camel's back.

One day after a long satisfying afternoon of pleasure, Jerry was getting dressed to go to visit his sister. Since we had already made plans to spend time together that evening I questioned him about it. He developed a fire in his eyes that I had never seen before. He walked up to me and hit me across my face. My first reaction was to swing in return. That turned out to be just what he wanted. He punched me in my face closed fist a couple of times as tears streamed down from my face. I couldn't believe what had just happened. I said "You are jumping on me because I want to spend time with you"? He didn't respond. I decided to let him go without further objection.

I spent the afternoon evaluating the situation. I was always told that you are supposed to leave a man that puts his hands on you, but since I had a poor record when it came to sustaining a relationship and I really didn't want to be alone again I reasoned that maybe he was just going through something and that it would never happen again.

But it wasn't long before the monster in him surfaced again. It was like he had an abundance of testosterone overflowing at every opportunity.

Not long after that he was let go from his job and didn't seem too enthusiastic about finding another one. Then his truck got repossessed. One day we were going somewhere in my car, he was darting in and out of traffic. He was speeding and ended up crashing into the car in front of us. He convinced me to sit in the front seat since he had previous driving offenses on his record. The guy in the other vehicle expressed opposition to his decision and a fight was about to ensue. Luckily the police got there before the first punch landed, although he did swing. He was like a ticking time bomb. The car was totaled and we ended up riding the bus. I still refused to heed the warning signals.

I guess I was so enthralled in the sexual escapades that I was blinded by the reality that there was no way that this partnership would have a happy ending. We were now consumers of public transportation. Once while waiting for the bus we went behind the bushes for a rendezvous. I had on a sundress which made for easy access. He slid my panties to the side and I bent over in anticipation of the ride. The fear of getting caught by someone walking by or exiting the building behind us only made the episode that much more thrilling.

I tooted my rear towards the sky. He grabbed my buttocks and pumped like there was no tomorrow. We saw the bus approaching and had to get to the finale. We came together and together we walked up to the bus stop as if nothing had ever happened. We simply climbed aboard with the other waiting passengers, only I couldn't help but twist, attempting to hold in all that he had released inside of me. We sat next to each other, held hands and attempted to control our breathing. When we made eye contact we both smiled.

Once we got home we had plans of just chilling. Jerry freshened up and went to the den where he was jamming to some smooth stepping sounds. I entered the room freshly showered, infused with the alluring fragrance of honey vanilla oil scrub. He inhaled the aroma and it's like his body exuded an aura resembling an inferno. This particular evening he was definitely on the prowl. In his deep voice he said "Damn baby, you are turning me on like Whoa"!!! His words spontaneously ignited a fire inside of me as well. Me, being a cougar, the thought of that simply drove me wild.

I dropped down to the floor and began to crawl seductively in his direction. His erection was visible. I instantaneously became moist. In that moment i was enticed to the point of exploding right then and there. As I got closer he moaned "Umm". He asked me to remove my baby doll bottoms. I did. He smiled. Then he asked me if I would hand him his drink that was sitting across the room. I attempted to rise when he said "Please continue to crawl". I obliged his wishes. I turned around and lowered my waist tooting my ass high into the air, allowing my snatch to speak volumes; voicing a yearning, her desire for action; for immense satisfaction. I looked back and teasingly licked my bottom lip as he stared with his mouth open.

Then like a lion he growled and pounced on me like a predator attacking his prey. He dove in face first, tantalizing my clitoris passionately. He was serious. No teasing only pleasing; devouring my sweet honey greedily like feasting at a buffet. In the midst of my heavenly indulgence I heard him growl again. I purred an immaculate release.

He turned me over and entered deep inside me, hitting even more spots. My pussy pulsated to the background sounds of neo soul. I grabbed his shoulders and he went in deeper. He began moving faster, breathing heavily and thrusting harder. I massaged his shoulders and back firmly with the balls of my fingers then I began grabbing, clawing and scratching with my nails. That must have really turned him on because he began to beat it up like a beast. We humped and bumped and rocked and rolled until we couldn't hold out any longer. We ooo'd and ahh'd in unison and exhaled with multiple exclamation points. We shivered electric convulsions then passed out right there on the floor for a few hours.

We were exhausted as we got up to shower. We soaped each other up and got turned on all over again. Round two was about to begin. We had such a synergy that we tapped into reserved energy to enjoy the magic of making love in the shower. The warm water soothed us for what seemed like hours. We released and cleansed again, then finally retired to the bed. At that particular moment we viewed the bed as our best friend as we smiled and fell off into a coma-like sleep.

As I mentioned before, we had smoked PCP a couple of times, wet daddies were what they were called on the streets. It always seemed to make everything slow down. For example, if we were walking down the block which would only take a few minutes, it would feel like it was taking hours. Once after smoking one we decided to make love. Everything seemed to be moving in slow motion except for Anita Baker's song "You Bring Me Joy"; for some reason that song seemed to end very quickly. We both enjoyed it and we put a pause on the action to backtrack to the beginning of the song. We did that about three or four times before we decided to let it play. Otherwise we would have never been able to take care of business, and of course that was the main mission at hand.

Disregarding that particular song I continued to ride him like a raging bull in a rodeo competition. He firmly grabbed my booty as he thrust his rock hard pole deep into the abyss of passion surrounding it. My body released like never before. I climaxed so long and hard that it was like a flowing waterfall. Afterwards he jumped up to take a shower.

I rolled over embracing a feeling of shame and confusion; not at some deep seated notion that women shouldn't enjoy sex to the extent of men. I was embarrassed because my subconscious mind, in spite of being overwhelmed by the use of embalming fluid was at the time well aware of the fact that I was lacing him with a golden shower. I felt confused as to why my conscious didn't override my decision to continue. I wasn't on any R Kelly stuff but in all honesty, it did feel good. Now I had to deal with the embarrassment of facing him. Also hoping he wouldn't be offended and angry since we did have a few more physical fights after the first one. And he definitely had to have realized what had happened.

When he returned to the bedroom I couldn't make eye contact. He said "You pissed on me". I looked up at him and quickly looked back down. I said nothing. I got up to run myself some bath water. I had planned to soak for a while. As I was sitting there in the tub contemplating what had happened, I realized that he wasn't angry, thank God. I don't think he was interested in a repeat performance though; for that matter neither was I. I guess he was just stating a fact. I decided right then that I would never again partake of that particular drug.

As time moved on, I wasn't really sure what was going on but Jerry had begun to spend more and more time at his sister's house. And his behavior was becoming more and more erratic. I also had begun to think he was having an affair, and I truly didn't care. In all honesty I had begun to enjoy his absence. I had become a nervous wreck, feeling like I had to always tip-toe on eggshells in my own home.

One afternoon he was getting dressed to go to his sister's house and invited me to join him. I wasn't too anxious to join him but I didn't want to start any confusion since lately it didn't take much to tick him off. So I got dressed and went along with him.

Once we arrived, his sister had a friend there and they all had a look about them. It was soon apparent that they were planning to smoke cocaine. This explained a lot of things about the way he had been behaving, but in my mind I knew that it didn't excuse the abuse I had been taking.

I had previously locked him out of the house one time. He told me if I didn't let him in that he was going to kill himself. I said then he would just be dead. Then he said he would kill me. I said well he would have to catch me. Then he said that he would hurt someone in my family. His words frightened me. All I could think about was my younger siblings, nieces and nephews. I believed him and didn't want to call his bluff.

I had also thought about enlightening family members of my situation but refrained for fear that they would seriously hurt Jerry and end up spending time in prison. I couldn't live with that thought either. Besides I didn't want to see anyone hurt. I just wanted to live a drama-free, peaceful existence. I spoke to God regularly for guidance to achieve the freedom I so dearly desired.

We were all in his sister's room as they passed the pipe around. I had vowed never to try it but when he passed it to me, he gave me a look like I had better do it or else. His family always did look at me as if I were stuck up. I was usually quiet around them because I would be entertained by their shenanigans. Anyway I took a couple of pulls. I felt a mellow high and was thinking to myself "Is this what all the hoopla is about"? They continued to buy more and more. When they asked me if I had any cash I gave them three dollars. His sister's friend seemed to be catering this affair.

When she ran out of money they all had a look of desperation on their faces. Jerry asked me once more did I have anything to offer. I responded "No". In actuality I had gotten paid early that week and had over four hundred dollars in my sock. I dared not mention it because I was sure that they would have beaten me down and took every penny. My mind was racing. I wasn't comfortable and wanted to leave ASAP. I was also confused, because I felt like there wasn't a high in the world that would make me spend my rent money. The friend began to develop tears as she said she had spent her grocery money and didn't know how she was going to feed him for the next month. His sister headed out to the neighbors to borrow loose change to ante up on another bag. Everyone there looked pathetic to me and I said I was about to leave. He stayed in hopes that someone else would stop by to contribute to continuing the party.

I was too threw. Since he didn't seem to mind me leaving, I was gone with the quickness. He stayed there and I went home to pack his stuff. I had 911 on speed dial because I knew he would act a fool when I told him that it was over. I didn't care about his threats either. I just wanted out.

He didn't return for two days and when he did I informed him of my plans to end our combustible relationship. Not only did he have no intentions of leaving but he commenced to violently beating me. I fought back but he got the best of me. He pinned me down on the floor and began choking me. The more I struggled, the more I could feel myself losing the ability to breathe.

Suddenly I heard a soft voice whisper in my ear "Stop fighting". I didn't understand how that would work but I decided to listen. I felt it was worth a try. I dropped my shoulders in surrender. He released the hold he had on my neck. I jumped up and ran to the bathroom. I had multiple red marks around my neck. I came out yelling "You Could Have Killed Me"! He said "if I wanted to kill you, you would be dead". I said "God saved my life. You had nothing to do with it".

He acted as if he was upset that I didn't give him credit for letting me go. As he lunged towards me this time, I happen to reach over and grab a hammer that I had been hanging pictures with earlier. I swung it with every ounce of power I had within my body. I was determined after seeing the red marks on my neck that I wasn't taking anymore ass whippings.

He fell to the floor. I called 911. He just laid there lifeless. I had hoped he wasn't dead. I didn't want that on my conscience. But at the same time I was proud of myself for taking control of the situation.

He didn't die that evening, but he will probably never be the same. His motor skills were stalled but other than that he can function normally. My family was surprised to hear of the situation since I had kept a tight wrap on my experiences. They were happy that it all worked out and that I had survived all the turmoil.

I spend many hours wondering if I had ever loved him. I sometimes even played the tune "Thin line between love and hate" attempting to attain some clarity. I realize now that love never entered the picture, it was sheer lust; the old bait and switch. Yeah, I was taken for a ride but I survived and blossomed like a rose growing from concrete.

I moved to another state and earned a college degree. I am now a counselor for battered women. I also recently got married to a wonderful man whom I took the time to get to know before becoming intimate. We have a son and hopefully a daughter on the way.

I realized that I don't have to live my life on the edge to enjoy it. And even though Jerry and I did have some adventurous sex, it wasn't worth dying for.

About Pat "Trishvision" Brown

Pat Trishvision Brown, a Chicago native currently residing in Minnesota. Creativity is my passion. All aspects...music, poetry, art, etc. I believe expression is liberating. And I am grateful as well as excited for the opportunity to be included in this awesome endeavor.

Role Reversal
by Thornne E. Xaiviantt

The world is full of two things, questions and answers. Growing up as a black female in Detroit Michigan most questions revolved around a murder scene or drugs. Nobody seemed to be able to answer questions unless it was related to these two subjects. Sad really...but I am here to tell you that when someone gets curious enough things can get shaken up really quick. My name is Mahogany Jianna Rhaines. In 27 years of life I have had both the privilege and in more ways than one struggled to obtain the answer to one in particular which is "What exactly is my role in this world?" I asked my mother this very question at the tender age of 7. I remember this cold blank stare beaming through heroine induced eyes. "Child? What the hell are ya talking about? huh? huh?" The source of what should be everything positive for a growing young girl was in fact the exact opposite.

This is something I would learn extremely quickly. I was the youngest of four children. I had three brothers. Two were gunned down before my very eyes in an alley and the third? Well....that is a mystery in itself. I do know that he was the oldest and has been missing for several years to this day. We were all two years apart in age so he would be 33 right now. Anyway, my mother and I had very few conversations. She stayed high and strung out most the time so intimate moments were very rare. I do remember one moment that stayed with me well into my adult years. She told me a disturbing story about an experience she had as a little girl. At the time, I was just fourteen years old. I always thought there were certain things a parent didn't discuss with their kids. However my mother always said that what you see in the streets of this world is nowhere worse than what your ears can hear.

She lit a cigarette and as she began to tell me the story, she laid back slowly coughing out a puff of smoke into the old gray sofa chair which housed her decaying thin frame. "Now...you aren't too young to hear this so when I tell you little girl don't go around telling folks that I did something bad do you hear me?" "Yes," I said with shaking pupils. I wasn't sure what to expect as I sat there legs Indian style on the floor focused at full attention. She started out telling me about the influx of drugs and high crime that plagued the city during her childhood. She went on to tell me how she was the product of a rape as well as her two sisters Gina and Rhiannon. Bitter details escaped her lips and tears fell from her quivering eyes as if she were re-living these horrible tragedies all over again. My mother wasn't the emotional type and since I didn't have my brothers around me now understand why both she and I have trouble connecting to men.

I was hesitant to ask but I mentioned that she never spoke of my stepfather. She kept old Polaroid's of him in photo albums and rarely let them out of her sight. I never told her but I would almost walk in on her at times. She set there weeping softly as she turned the pages slowly with the plastic rubbing against her finger tips as she looked through each album. My only escape from such misery believe it or not wasn't the streets but school. It wasn't hard to figure out one simple concept. The only way out of the ghetto was to arm yourself with a smart brain and drive to get out. I was an honor roll student. I thought of the letter A as "A way out" I strived for straight A's and succeeded graduating from high school within the top percentile of my class. I'm not sure how I made it in such a fashion considering I never slept well on school nights or any other. The sounds of gunfire, screams, sirens, and of course the front door moving throughout the night were indeed the reason among others. I didn't have many friends in school but I did have one friend that I was pretty close to.

Her name was Sha'nelle. I called her Shay. Shay's dad was on the police force as a member of the Narcotics Unit. One day Shay told me that she wanted to bring her dad to career day. We were seniors in high school at the time. I remember this day because the event was held in the gymnasium and when you get 800 high school kids in the same space anywhere near the police it's usually not a good thing. Career day brought various occupations including doctors and lawyers as well as veterinarians and carpenters. My interest was in Shay's dad though. He talked about the mental aspect of his job more so than the typical war stories on the streets. I was very intrigued as I listened to him speak. He asked if there were any questions at the end of his presentation. I raised my hand and asked. "How do I become an officer?" A pen dropped and silence swept across the entire gym. He looked at me and said. "You must be 21, a high school graduate, no felonies, and pass written as well as physical fitness tests. You also need a year in the academy to train with an officer then you're in from there." We just received report cards that day and little did he know I didn't care about people staring I wanted in. I walked down the bleachers breeching the wall of staring eyes as I made my way to him. I handed him my report card my medal for honor roll with an application already filled out.

He looked at me and said "Oh my goodness...ummm...wow...you're really a smart kid." I look at him and said "Don't forget serious" He paused briefly and said "Meet me at the corner of Broadway and Chestnut in the Hard Rock Cafe tomorrow afternoon. Bring what is on this list." He shook my hand and that was it. Shay walked up to me laughing. "Giiiiiiirl the whole gym is looking at you like the town snitch what's up?" I looked at her in slight disgust "Look you know this is my dream and why. You of all people should understand that this is personal. I want to find my brother and find out what my mother isn't telling me." Shay stared at me hard.

"You....you mean who murdered your brothers?" It took everything I had not cry in that moment. "Yes...now can we go? Besides I have a date with your dad" I laughed as she punched me in the shoulder. The next day came quick and I was in and out the shower, dressed, and as I stuck a warm pop tart in my mouth my cell phone buzzed. It was Shay's crazy butt. "Hey girl what's up?" "Hey bestie my dad is already at the Cafe waiting for you. I wanted to wish you luck today. I told him that you are really serious about this cop thing and you know I talked you up right?" I laughed and smiled. "Thanks Shay I appreciate this. Now let me go so I can get there to meet him" "Okay girl and don't be trying to hit on my dad either or else we will have to knuckle up ha ha ha ha" "Bye silly!" I hung up and grabbed my purse and the black folder sitting on the old wood nightstand by my bed.

An hour later I arrived at the cafe. I saw her dad in the window and he waved me in. "Hi I see you are punctual too that's a good thing" he said smiling. "Here, I ordered you some food. My daughter said this is your favorite" I was so nervous but I kept reminding myself to be calm. "I brought this with me" I handed him the black folder. He opened it and skimmed over the documents. "Mmmm...nice....four point grade average....cum laude graduate....cheerleader...soccer captain four years....team player...leadership...brains....well well, I'm impressed." What kind of shape are you in kid? "I ran with the basketball and football teams during their camps sir. My fastest mile run is under six minutes I'm flexible and I'm pretty good with a gun. I took marksmanship classes as electives. I can hit a coke can sixty yards out with a be be gun." Hmmm a be be gun hun? ha ha ha okay okay." Well tell you what? You have to go through the preliminaries just like all the others before you. I won't lie to you it's no walk in the park especially here in Detroit. The department and academy testing process is hell and not too many women pass it.

Are you certain you want to do this? If I put you in the
rotation for testing and you pull out I look bad so let me
know now" I looked him dead center in the eyes as if I
was going to snipe him with a rifle. "Yes...I'm ready
right.....nooooooow." Three years passed and I was on
my own beat I had my own squad car and of course my
own set of tools. The Gloc the night stick pepper spray,
you name it I was packing it. I was ready to serve and
protect the very neighborhood that had shot at me
stabbed me and took my brother's life. I did so with
great success and after two additional years I had
proven myself to enter the Narcotics division and guess
who my boss was...the very man who helped me five
years ago. Sha'nelle's dad Lt Bradley Masters.
"Well...well...I look at my roster and who do I see?"
Mahogany J Rhaines...wow.....nice....well I would say
welcome rookie but you've earned the right to be called
a fellow agent. Narcotics agent to be exact. This is not
for the weak and since you made it here I'm safe
assuming that you are ready for your first assignment.
Too soon? Yes? No?" I looked at him and said. I didn't
come this far to back down sir" Well little did I know he
was testing me for about a year and I didn't know it. My
beat was right in the heart of drug traffic central and
Detroit was the prostitution capital of Michigan at the
same time.

Lt Masters walked me into the briefing room. And sat
me down. Okay here is the deal we have a serious
prostitution ring going on here in the city and we need
you undercover. These people are not only sexing for
cash but they are being strung out on everything under

the kitchen sink in the process. I have two other officers set to be with you but I need you to penetrate this ring and bust it up so the department can bring this shit to a screeching halt. I don't care how you do it get creative and be swift." That's all he had to say because within six months I had my own shit set up and made busts in the process.

Being creative was the key. You see I was undercover which meant blending in and since people remembered me from the hood I had to change the very game I was trying to end. I started my own business. You see I was the pimp and I made about twenty men twenty fine as whine men my hoes. They brought me drugs as well as money but most importantly information. Cocaine, crack, heroine, speed, marijuana, ecstasy pills, it was like the supermarket of the drug world. I had taken over a lot of turf in just a short time.

However there was one problem I never expected to come into play. Love is one of the sneakiest and powerful things. I was standing at a rendezvous point waiting for my inside man to bring me a shipment and intel on a bust we were close to making. The block I was on is small so people tend to stand out. I watched someone who was watching me. This tall brother stood maybe six yards across the way standing maybe 6"6 about 230 lbs. Mmmph I had mind fucked him already without knowing him. My clit stood at attention as he slowly approached me. "Excuse me.....word on the street says you are running shit around here am I right? At first I was a little apprehensive but his smile was like a tractor beam pulling me in. "What are you looking for brotha? A fuck a buck? Or what?" I said snapping the bubble gum in my mouth. "Confident I see nice...." he says smiling back at me.

His gray alluring eyes seeped sexiness all over the damn place. "Well I need cash. I don't have a job, I have a daughter who has an empty stomach. I lost my job a few ago when I was voted out of a law firm that I was supposed to be a partner in" he said with a sad face. "Lawyer? Really? What's a lawyer doing around here making street money when you are accustomed to legit money?" "That was five long years ago sweetie. It's been longer than that since I've had sex." I was stunned. It wasn't going to be any longer if he kept touching my hand the way he was. Mmmmmph I almost forgot what I was supposed to be doing for a moment.

Okay so you want cash? Well I run a tight ship around here and that means no receiving without earning. I have twenty other men on my crew they average 600 Benjamin's a night sometimes more. I get twenty percent of anything below that and forty percent of anything past a stack do the math. Depending on your hustle as well as how good you smuggle or fuck you may make it in my business are we straight?" He smiled and said "yes" Wooooo shit I couldn't concentrate. Damn he was fine as hell! I had to report in to the lieutenant in twenty minutes so I cut the conversation short. "Look I gotta make this pickup, call me at this number in about two hours and we will talk. What's your name dude?" I said trying not to sound turned on. "Aaron.....and yours?" he said winkin at me. "Mahog....I mean...uh...you just know me as the boss alright? Two hours...call....not a minute before or later...deuces..." I quickly walked away slowly pulling out my radio once I was out of view asking my officer to meet me inside the storage unit facility a block up the street. Ten minutes later my informant shows up breathing hard as hell. "What the...what's wrong Sergeant? Talk to me." He managed to catch his breath and collect himself a few seconds later. "I was.....I was....was.... making the pickup for you and got into a fight with one of the suppliers. He punched me so I fought back. All over the count of the product."

I was pissed. "Shit sergeant....if this blows my case and all the work we've done to this point that's my ass and yours do you understand that?" I was absolutely livid. Look you gotta protect yourself but we have put a lot on the line and put too much into this to cave in. Look, I'm trying to get a couple more guys in the ring and that will be enough to make my plan work more smoothly.

Go get cleaned up and back to the diner on Sixth Street. See what you can find out there. I heard that some key players are having dinner there in an hour or so." He left and that was that. My cell phone buzzed and I already knew who it was. "Yes Lieutenant? Yes....things are okay but one of my guys had a run in with a supplier. Yes...Yes sir I understand sir. Alright....10/4." Ugggghh.....what the hell? I was tired hungry and pissed. This was not a good combination at all. Two hours later my hoes were starting to blow up my other cell. I told all of them to meet at the usual spot. I managed to get a warehouse on the block as a meeting place. I did all my transactions and counts there.

My prostitution business was booming. I didn't have any busts but I did have evidence to put folks away for a long time. I gave all my men the usual speech and collected my percentages of the night's profits. Afterward, I knew it was time to get some shut eye. I had to be careful not to be followed back to my apartment. This was a dangerous game and word of mouth says I was on many hit lists from rival ring leader's mob bosses. I noticed a private call on my personal cell. I usually don't answer private calls but something prompted me to answer this one. "Hello?" The voice on the other end was raspy but familiar. "Meet me at the diner on sixth and magnolia tonight....alone...I have information for you." I stood there silent for a moment. "Who is this?" I said curious. "Now...now...no questions just yet. Meet me tonight...sit in the back inside a booth. I'll see you before you see me....don't be late 8p.m. sharp"

I was very alarmed because not too many people had my personal cell number. I was hoping it would just be a wrong number but whoever it was spoke as if he knew me. I put my phone a down and proceeded to get undressed and took a much needed shower. That voice......it was oh so familiar yet perplexing at the same time. I lathered my tired aching frame head to toe. Ten minutes later, after my shower, I put on my lace black panties with matching bra. I put on a black T shirt as well. I reach in the top drawer of my night stand brandishing my Gloc 25 police issued pistol. I loaded the clip with fifteen hollow point rounds and engaged the safety. Once I loaded the clip in, I placed it right next to my head for easy access as I lay there thinking of the man I hired tonight. His touch haunted the confines of my nerve ending's tiniest hiding places. I closed my eyes at the thought of those addicting eyes and alluring lips. He stood tall and my sleepy fantasy took refuge in the drowsy crevices of my sex driven imagination.

My nipples were erect causing me to be restless and bothered. I felt moist sensations in between my softened thighs as I contemplated erogenous acts of pure sensual satisfaction with this man I only knew as "Aaron" There was this aura about him....a powerful vibe I couldn't shake. I laid there in my bed drowning in his possibility. I wasn't sure exactly why I was feeling this way. I don't know a thing about him other than the brief conversation we had. So why did I need his touch so badly? Maybe I was starving for something that I had not had since my first high school boyfriend of years past. Connection to the outside world was limited because of my work so maybe my body was just over reacting. Although I didn't quite understand the nature of what I was feeling, it felt so good to me.

The nature of this work is so sensitive keeping your personal and business separate is indeed challenging. I often wonder how people keep it together. What is the secret? I guess everyone is different. Oh.....well I guess I will figure it out as I go. As I closed my eyes, I drifted off into a blissful sleep. The next morning I was awakened by the sound of my cell phone going off. I looked at the number and it was my boss calling. "Hello?" I said with sleep filled eyes. "Yes...things are going as planned and I should have a report for you by the end of the week.

No....not yet, I haven't made contact with the supplier yet.

Okay....okay....alright....thanks Lieutenant take care...."
Sssshhh...I swear if I didn't love my job and need it I would stop kissing his butt all the time. The thing with undercover work is that you sometimes lose your place between the world you are paid to live in at times and the world you have no choice to live in all the time. I set up on the bed pushing my hair back wondering. "What the hell is going to happen today?" Once again asking questions in my brain that seemed to cry out for answers. I put on my favorite stone wash jeans and white tank top. I decided a bun was my best hairdo. I had a feeling the day was going to be a rough one. I was usually right when I had this feeling too. I stood on my feet after tying my shoes and then strapped on my Gloc. I grabbed two extra clips and my jacket. I walked out the door letting a slow breath out trying to prepare for what this day would bring. I got into my candy apple red 2012 Mitsubishi Lancer Evolution and started the beast within.

The turbo charger chimed in as I revved the engine one time like I always do. Thanks to some aftermarket modifications and a lot of overtime I was able to transform my car from 280 factory ponies to 550 pulse pounding thoroughbred horses of fast and furious performance. I sped off to my place of "business" quickly passing the 60mph mark within 4 seconds. I arrived at the designated warehouse ten minutes later and parked just a half block from the building. I didn't want anyone making out my vehicle for obvious reasons. I stepped and walked down to the warehouse feeling for my Gloc to ensure that it was tight in the holster. I slipped the two extra clips onto my belt and zipped up my jacket. I had no idea what was in my immediate future but signals would soon come very quickly. I walked in to find everyone standing around waiting on me. "How was the night?" I said with a focused face. "Not so good, business wasn't anywhere near what it was just a week ago."

A voice boomed from the back. I just stared at the metal table supporting the small stacks of cash in front of me. "Hmmmm....looks like you guys need to hustle more. When I take my cut you will have to have more hustle unless you don't plan on eating that day" The life of a pimpstress is one I never understood. I was totally in control and part of me loved it. Now I know how the lieutenant feels when he has us standing for roll call at five in the morning. I grabbed the stacks of money counting the old torn bills as I thought to myself what my strategy would be. I needed more information than what I had in order to meet my lieutenant's demands. I was too far in not to have more so I couldn't really argue.

I handed everyone their cut of the stash and just as I did so my phone began to buzz. I looked at it and it was a private number but something told me the voice on the end would be quite familiar. "Hello?" I said softly. "Hey....it's me....Aaron.....ummm....I couldn't be out there tonight. There is so much going on right now. I am calling you because I need to see you." I paused to catch my breath. "Well....you know where I am so why not

come out?" He sat there quiet for a moment.
"Well...can we meet away from the warehouse....this is
really personal for me and I don't want the others to
know what's going on. Can you pick me up too? My car
isn't running so well either." I normally had no
"business" partners in my ride but my hormones told
me otherwise. "Okay I will be there in fifteen minutes
you need to be ready in ten understood?" Aaron paused
briefly "Yes....yes ma'am". I rounded up the paperwork
on the table and went to into the small office to lock up.
I keyed in the code tothe building alarm on the wall
closing the office door. I immediately closed the
creaking door and quickly exited before the motion
sensor beams activated. I jumped in my car snapping
my seat belt on and put the key in the ignition. I turned
the key as the engine boomed to life I peeled backwards
and then as i shifted, the car launched forward.
Screaming down the street, I could feel the power of
the dual cam turbo charged beast underneath roar. I
loved my car. Sometimes it was an orgasm on wheels.

Within ten minutes, I was in the Victory park district
which was a rougher part of the downtown area. I kept
my GLOC close to me, because the number of officer
casualties had doubled in the last two years. Forty
percent occurring in the same area I'm driving in right
now. "Keep calm....relax....just focus." Kept telling
myself that but my nerves were on a different page. I
looked closely through my windshield noticing a figure
standing under a light post a few yards ahead. The
closer I got to the light on my right, I recognized the
person. It was indeed Aaron. I pulled over to the curb

unlocking the door for him. "Get in Hurry" He eased in closing the door with an odd look on his face. "What's the matter Aaron?" I don't normally pick up my guys in my car but I'm sticking my neck out for you this one time so make it good" I had no idea what I was saying but he would certainly prove to be a good listener because what happened afterward totally changed my life. "I need you to drive me somewhere." I was a little thrown off by his tone but decided entertain his request. "Where? Aaron?"

He didn't give me a straight answer but I made an exception. "Just take the bypass and follow it down about three miles or so. I will tell you where to go from there." I did as he asked and it seemed like both of us were confused because there wasn't much conversation the entire ride. Fifteen minutes later we arrived at this hotel. I recognized it immediately because I had made a bust in the area about a year ago. "Why are we at a..." He covered my mouth gently and motioned for me to exit the car. I was completely stunned. Aaron stepped out carrying a small bag with him. "Come in with me, the room is already registered and paid for I just didn't have a ride." We walked up to a first floor door marked "103". As we entered there was a familiar incent type smell in the room. "Aaron what's going on?" He whispered something I will never forget. "You, you're a cop" I was completely stunned. "Since we first met I knew it but didn't want to give you away. Plus the way you move the way you talk...it's a dead giveaway. My mother and father both were cops. Both in Narcotics just like you. That's in fact why we never got along because when I lost my job at the firm, my wife left me after setting me up, my parents never used their connections to help their only child. I hated cops after that." But you....you are different....somehow someway....you are different." Aaron moved closer and I wanted to reach for my gun but I froze. He took my hand with that powerful touch....and my knees started to wobble slowly. Aaron....I.....I...." He removed my belt and weapon with one hand caressing my waist with the other. "If you want to arrest me fine then I confess. I have used drugs in the past....I have even took food to feed my daughter, but I brought you here tonight because I have been holding something more intense back. I have been attracted to you from day one night one all the above. However....I only ask that if I give you what's in my possession, then you must give me my heart's desire if only for tonight." I looked at him as he stepped away from me. He picked up the bag which he laid on the dresser and opened it. He pulled out a white envelope and removed documents and photos. "Here..." he said softly. "There you will find all the major players in this game you entered. Every kingpin and his or her connections. Every hideout, every alias, DNA samples, the entire case you are working on has already been solved." I did the work for you." I was dumbfounded because everything was there. This evidence could make my career for sure." I looked at him strangely. "What is it you want from me?" I said nervously. He took the envelope out of my hand slowly putting the papers and photos inside and whispered. "You....just for tonight....you....right here....right now......I want you..." I turned away to walk to my gun but he pulled me toward him spinning me around quick. "Tell me you don't feel an attraction....." He went to kiss me quickly and I was lit a blaze by his fiery kiss. My knees buckled at his passionate aggression. He pulled me tighter into his somewhat muscular frame removing my earrings and I found myself taken in the moment. I removed my jacket and shirt quickly and he dropped my belt and pants with even quicker speed. I removed his shirt with reckless motion and planted my own fire-filled kiss on his chest and both shoulders. He gripped my small waist hoisting me in the air to the queen size bed two feet away. Once planted there on my back Aaron mounted me slow gazing at me like a lion that hadn't eaten in months.

My legs took a mind of their own spreading slowly underneath his slow heaving breaths. His manhood tapped my clitoris with authority and my wetness quivered down my inner thighs. He leaned closer kissing me and my abdomen sank under his muscular six pack. "mmmm...." the moan seeped out of my breath-taken vocal cords. Caressing my back with his left hand he then placed with his right that erect monster knocking the door down of my pussy like a porn swat team.

I received his entry welcoming him with a slight upward thrust of my own. His low grunt let me know that this was definitely going to be barn burner. He snapped bra loose with one hand to my surprise and removed it from the front with his teeth! "Skilled I see...." I whispered. Aaron took the offensive diving deeper into my pool of wetness. Driving deeper and deeper I wept in epic nerve bending pleasure as he ravaged my insides. My legs shook with every pulse pounding thrust. "YEEEESSSS!" I shouted as he found my G-SPOT with ease. "I want you...." He whispered as he pushed deeper into my core. I responded with a heavy grip of his waist pulling him in as far as I could. My juices drowned his shaft as we moved in unison to a passionate motion I had never felt before. He stopped suddenly, backed out, and gripped me around the waist, turning me over. He pulled my ass north and entered like a homeless wild dragon. "Mmmmm.....AAAARRROOONNN!" My clit swollen to its max at the continuous onslaught of his ball bashing aggression. For forty five heart racing minutes he thrashed and as I came profusely soaking the sheets time and time again, I literally gasped for air as he began to breath heavily as well. "I want you.....I need you....." he exclaimed with heavy lungs as I felt his warm love liquid fill my hot center. He pushed three more time releasing his seed into me with each push. He released his grip and then turned me over. I was left on my back with blurred vision.

My heart finally reached a normal beat as my vision slowly cleared. To my surprised he slowly dressed himself and handed me my clothes. "I know we just broke just about every rule that contains letters. I know what you are looking for and thanks to connections I have from my old job, I was able to find you in this operation. I wanted to see if you could help me if I helped you. I sat there stunned and slowly realized what a compromised position I was in. "If you help me get back into the district attorney's office I will gladly hand over all this evidence to you. If you turn me in for prostitution or drugs or whatever else this ring of theirs is involved with you will never see this envelope again. I need you...please help me...." I sat there totally baffled and undecided. Here I was thinking I had things under control on the outside all the while forgetting to control my hormones and now look at me....I am caught in the most bizarre role reversal and have no clue how to get out. The question that has yet to be answered...How do I reverse my own reversal? hmmmm.........

"Sin 'Sations"
by Thornne E. Xaiviantt

What is this?

Am I dreaming?

Forehead steaming

My clothes start slippin'

I must be trippin'

Oh I can feel those hands grippin"

A glimpse of imagination?

What is this?

Such an incredible inevitable "sin'sation"

I feel so used

My body is amused

Hormones tamed at mere thoughts construed

Nerve endings subdued

Dancing and prancing around

Perplexed as I'm being sexed by euphoric sounds

I feel so guilty as hordes of "sin'sation" rumble within me

My soul takes off aimlessly shamelessly running on empty

Mmmm...sssshh...yes...thats the place....

As I smile is it worthwhile?

Is the "sin'sation" written all over my face?

Or has pure ecstasy blown me away without a trace?

Thump..thump...bump..bump...oh my my my

I couldn't win against innocence at all up against this wall

No matter how hard I try

This feeling this presence wrapped around my essence

A sign of sure tampering with my body's evidence

Lines crossed as my body is embossed and glossed

I found a new feeling once thought to be lost

I find myself running back again...again....and again

You ask how did I make this determination.

The truth is I understand why the "sin" comes before the sation.

I chase my breath recklessly

This "sin'sation"" erupts perspiration

Pleasure dominating me effortlessly

I drown in joy

Temptation gets the best of me

I close my eyes at "sin'sation"s end

As pure bliss consumes the rest of me.......

"Sacred Place"
by Thornne E. Xaiviantt

Searching the deepest crevices of human boundary

Curiosity leading your mind to grip every feeling around me

Your mental penetrates my deepest thoughts defense

Oh so intense

The conversation

Unbelievable coincidental mental stimulation

Heartbeats tangled in flesh pounding fashion

Two sets of eyes locked in a gaze.

I'm so amazed please don't let this feeling fade

Twists in unison with turns as our bodies yearn

Fire ignited by desire as the passion continues to burn

Feverish pitch is reached as restraint is breeched

Cries of "more" lead the charge as love is unleashed in the sheets

Kisses pave the way to a tantalizing embrace

The search light is on...can you find my sacred place?

I need you but simultaneously tease you and lead you

You starve for passion so I feed you....

Oh...Oh....Oh...yes....yeeeeees...I see you...

Buried within cerebral habitat imagine that....

A place so sensual spiritual subliminal

I touch every nook and crack....

Mmmmm...that was intentional...

No question it was consensual

I shudder at just the visual

A moment so pivotal

I am no longer empty

For your love is oh so plentiful

My sacred place has found comfort in you

I permit your passage

You wine and dine your way through

Like a thief in the night you already knew

I was never a secret

My body is the shrine which holds my heart

My sacred place was always with you......

About Thornne E. Xaiviantt

I am father to my beautiful 9 year old son Brayden. I am the youngest of my mother's 3 children. My passions are quite simple. I love the Martial Arts specifically Tae Kwon Do and Brazilian Jiu-Jitsu. My second passion is writing. I love to write constantly. I love short stories and poetry.

"I Touched Stars That Night..."
by Ebony Rose aka Latte Fally

I was in this mansion or castle or something...wandering the halls searching for something, someone perhaps...with a candle in my hand. Passed by so many rooms...so many twists and turns trying to find whatever it was I sought after... Then I came to this juncture where the hall split into four directions... I chose one and kept searching. Not too far after I made the turn... A shadow came lumbering out of the darkness...towering above me...startling me. The shadow grasps my shoulders and pulled me toward it...groping and feeling me as it did. The sensations consumed me quickly... I closed my eyes as I started to feel like a rag doll in its grasp...

I was pushed back against the wall feeling lips upon mine...gentle kisses then a tongue pressed through tasting my mouth... In my head I was thinking: Is this what I sought after? With every touch and kiss, I melted even more...still I grasped the candle in one hand...as if it read my thoughts the shadow grasped my hand that held the candle...taking it away and placing it on a nearby hall table... Whilst doing all that, it kept me pinned in place against the wall. I felt completely helpless...like I was under some spell or something...then I was jolted back to reality when the shadow kneeled down before me... I was trying to see who this shadow was in the faint light from the table...but could only make out the outline of its face...

As it kneeled, the shadow's hands hoisted up my nightgown... I felt a swift cool breeze as he did... rubbing my legs and thighs very gently as he parted them...at that moment, my breath was caught up in my throat... What was he doing? Can I escape from him before he continues? Then I felt lips on my inner thighs where its fingers had been before...lips that sweetly caressed my skin ever so softly... I felt myself giving in to him more and more... Then I panicked... I had no undergarments on...does he know this? Up to that point he hadn't touched me there to really know if I did or not... As if he read my thoughts, he lifted one leg up and came closer to me and stopped... I felt his warm breath blowing on my essence... I leaned further back on the wall as if I could disappear within it... I squirmed a bit knowing what was next... In one swift motion, he lifted my other leg onto his other shoulder... I was pressed against the wall with my legs over his shoulders... My pussy was exposed entirely...no escape. Then I felt his breathe getting warmer and warmer as I felt lips touch my nether ones. At that moment, I heard him moan...right then as his tongue lashed out and tasted me...

All I could do is moan softly feeling it probe my pussy waking her up... I felt his nose nudging my sensitive love bud as his tongue dove into my wet essence. I was trying to think of whom this could be...but even that thought was being drowned out by the strong tongued lashes that were causing me to moan louder...

I felt his hands on both cheeks of my buttocks as he pressed into my essence...then he did the inevitable. His tongue went straight to my clit, violently lashing... I moaned loudly as he attacked it...then I felt him suck it in... The pressure he applied was so intense I felt tears running down my face as he showed no mercy. I squirmed and squealed with complete solid pleasure! "Ooh yesss! Oooh yesss!" I exclaimed. The heat within me increased and increased... I felt myself soaring higher and higher... I touched stars that night. The licking and sucking continued... I heard him say my name between lashes... He licked me like I've never been licked before, conquering my territory clitorically. For a split second, I thought who was this man? And how the hell dost he know my name?

All that didn't really matter at the moment... He ravished and devoured my essence... rendering me listless still showing no mercy... felt my body surrendering to him... I wanted him to take me to a place where I've not been...make me leap from one ecstatic cloud to another... Then it happened... I couldn't hold it back... A sound from deep within escaped my mouth as the orgasm moved throughout my body...while this was occurring he showed no mercy as he suctioned my love bud harder making it feel even more wonderful. Oooh yess! I touched stars that night... I felt their heat showering down on me...sizzling as they caressed my skin...so way up high in the sky. My goodness! My body quaked with so many aftershocks...with him still latched onto my essence...like he wasn't going to let go until my body was spent and lifeless... leaned against the wall, with my legs over his shoulders, panting heavily and sweating profusely...

I whispered: "Who are you? Why have you done this to me? Do I know you? It seems you know me and by my name at that---who art thou?" He slowly lifts each of one of my legs from his shoulders...planting them on solid ground, yet still holding me as if he knew my legs were like putty and I couldn't stand on my own...

And without any warning, he swiftly turns me around pressing my body against the wall. He lifts up my gown and next I feel something warm and hot against my thighs. I realize that this man is about to probe my insides. With one swift thrust upward he is inside my honeyed walls. With each stroke I feel his hot and heavy breaths on the back of my neck. I can barely breathe as he dives higher and higher within my confines. Whoever he is at this moment I don't really care. He's making me feel so right and wanted, making me want to shout "I love you!" over and over again.

He grasps my hips as he plunges his thickness deeply into my pussy, making it seemingly drip as if it's crying out for more. Moans from my mouth hasten his rhythms as goes even deeper, no holds barred. My pussy muscles contract allowing his thick and hard phallus to evade what needed to be sated. My nails dig into the walls leaving clawed marks as if an angry beast did it. "Yes, yes, yes! Take it like it is yours! Give me all you have to give... make me yours!"

That made him go crazy and he starts grinding into me like I've never had it before. His began breathing heavier and heavier, groaning into my ear and nibbling my neck as his climax drew nearer. I pushed myself backward meeting his every thrust. We both were moaning arias that crescendo high into the heavens, we both touched stars that night. As we both descended back to our normal selves, he pulls down my gown straightening it and turn me around.

He reached over to get the candle...raising it higher to reveal his face. My ebony eyes widen as I finally saw his face... It was, was you!! Standing there ever so tall above me with your caramel complexion and those dimples that smile...hazel eyes beaming knowingly that you've conquered and overthrown my territory.

"Yes my sweet love, it is I..." He said with such a mischievous grin upon his handsome face. "I had to have you...leave my mark so that no other shall explore this of which is mine and mine alone..." He pulls me closer to him and leans down passionately kissing me...this time I kissed back with such fervor that an orgasm went through my body...then there was a loud thundering Boom! We both looked in the direction of the noise while still in each other's arms...it got louder and louder as it got closer...it was like we were glued to the spot and couldn't move...then...then...

I woke up...panting heavily looking around for him... "Where hast thou gone my love?" Tears stream down my face...heart heavy... I slowly roused myself...walking around the house looking for him...and then... I see him over there standing in front of the fireplace...all tall and handsome. I walk softly as not to disturb him...but the slight rustling of my nighty startles him and he turns around smiling...

"How did you sleep my love?" he asked as he motions me to come to him... "I did not want to disturb your slumber, so I left a while ago..."

"I slept pretty well...save for my dream...I guess it was a dream that we were together in a large hall...with you pleasuring me..." I said looking up into his eyes... "Was it a dream?"

"My love...no, that wasn't a dream at all...we were together a few hours ago in the great hall...then you fainted," he replied. "I had to carry you to the bedroom...you are feeling okay now yes?"

I stood there in his arms pondering... I fainted? "Well yes... I feel fine...just wondering what happened to make me faint."

"I don't know my sweet...just know you fainted and I was scared something bad happened to you. But you are fine and that's all that matters. I'm here with you and you are here with me..." he said as he takes my face into his hands and kisses me...

I started feeling really strange at that point...like something was tugging and pulling me away from him... he became something intangible that I could not hold onto... he faded away and out of sight...

"Garyyy... Garyyy!!" I yelled...but no answer came back...

I felt myself swirling around and around...then nothingness...

I sat up in my bed...alone...in the midst of the darkness and quiet still of the night...wind blowing outside my window...

The thumping of my heart and heavy breathing brings me back to true reality...feeling the dampness of the sheets around me... I sigh and then I smile...hugging my pillow tightly and thinking... A dream within a dream...

~The End... Or Is It? ~

~*EbonyRose y Lattè Fallz aka Latricia Mazyck*~

Reminded of the Fickle-Minded
by Ebony Rose aka Latte Fally

Why did you become so fickle?

You remember my fancy?

The one you use to tickle?

Made my nether regions so hot

and heavy, it trickled...

Down my thick thighs

'Cause you hit the right spot—

Making me bellow out moans and sighs...

Dug my nails into your

Caramelesqued creamy skin...

Looked into your chocolate-brown coloured eyes—

Heard your gruntin' and groanin'...

As my pubes tightened around your thickened phallic tool—

Bringing it like you were "True 'Ol Skool"...

I remember like it was yesterday—

A memory that will soon fade...

Your touch,

My touch...

Of my fingers through your curly locks—

the feel of your soft "cushiony lips" as our bodies rocked...

I remember the way you caressed my insides—

Made my valley rich and full of much nectar and honey...

Earth shattering moans that calmed

treacherous waters—

I do remember because the Earth moved that night...

I remember, do you remember?

What seemed like a lifetime ago,

was just a blotted vision of my yesterday

And you, I've already forgotten...

A "has been"—

I just wanted to remember when...

DJ's Bad Girl
by Ebony Rose aka Latte Fally

Hey Mr. DJ, you're playing my song,

Melodies reverberating

Sending vibrations down to the inside of my thong…

Strumming my Inner Mental, got me masturbating

Anticipating how much longer

I can suppress this heated thing

Inside me that's getting stronger…

Stronger as your music

Comes out the speakers in hushed tones

Making my body and soul get use to it—

Likened to quivering and quavering dancing bones…

Within my milk chocolate skin

I've become a vessel vexed by groovy

Muddled verse and rhyme, transfixed and mesmerized

Hips revolving 360°

Hands clapping and feet stompin'

Almost buckling knees…

Metamorphing unknowingly before my eyes,

Eyes glazed over as if under your symphonic spell—

Heat rising about to explode

As I fantasize of your erupting uprightness

Thy erection spewing into me your love-juiced load—

Do Re Mi Fa La Ti Do!

I sing out moan after moan,

As the lyrics climax in its own chorus...

Orgasmic gushing Arias escape my lips

Electric shockwaves spread through me

Inside and Outward to my fingertips...

Body trembling wave after wave

Sending rivulets of wetness down my legs

Heavy panting, sultry hot breaths...

As this Body calms down from the

Fever pitch you've caused—

Soft moans escape involuntarily

As I watch my reflection in the mirror;

Eyes looking back blinking listlessly

While the intense hot throbbing ebbs from my clit to my tits,

Slow down to small livid tremors—

That song has killed me softly...

Almost making me speak in tongues

Ever so sweetly,

Oui, oui mon cherie amour

C'est la vie

Voulez-vous avec moi mon ami?

The song fades out--

I calm down as the Moscato

I've been drinking slowly but surely put me to sleep...

Softly whispers, Mr. DJ you've played my song,

DJ's naughty bad girl is waiting--

So now come home and take off my dripping wet thong...

*About
Ebony Rose aka Latte Fally*

A Native of Myrtle Beach, South Carolina... My passion for writing started at an early age but didn't reach my full potential until about 10 years ago. I was highly encouraged to continue writing by very close friends and relatives. Since then, I've written mostly romantic and erotic poetry as well as short stories. First and far most, I give honor and glory to GOD for my beautiful gift of writing.

Apartment 13A
by Katrina Gurl

Missy Davis had a special way of handling her unhappy
marriage and she seriously hoped no one would ever
find out her enchanting secret. She'd throw herself 24-
7 into her novel writing and she loved every minute of
it. During any given day of the week she set up scenes
from one erotic adventure to the next.

On occasions she'd take her laptop to the nearest
Starbucks to openly express her hidden fantasies...well,
on paper, anyway and in her mind, some of the best
looking men had the leading roles in her assorted
ventures. Most of the men that featured in her stories
seemed to be just what she was attracted to in real life.
Average height to very tall, caramel to brown skinned
brothers' with good business sense, but also the natural
ability to handle himself on the streets.

***

There was a new guy that just moved in the apartment above Kimbella. The guy seemed like one of those quiet mysterious types, but he sure was easy on the eyes, nonetheless. He was very fit, about 6 feet tall, caramel completion and from what she could see as he greeted a few nosey neighbors coming in and out unloading a U-Haul truck with his things; he had a really great, healthy smile.

It was a Saturday so everyone seemed to be home watching ever single box he brought upstairs. He never broke not even one sweat and he only had one person helping him. Kimbella could surely notice that his youth was something that would attract her painfully. She most definitely wanted to meet him without coming off as nosy as her non-conspicuous neighbors.

At about noon Kimbella walked across the hall to get her mail. Of course she timed it perfectly for the moment he was entering the quant brownstone with another box. After retrieving her mail and locking the box again, she notices all she really had was a bunch of junk mail, but as she noticed the new guy getting closer towards her...she acted like she was looking down at very important mail and bumped into the guy.

"Oh my God...I'm so sorry! How clumsy am I???" The new guy almost dropped the heavy box filled with electronics, but his agility was so on point that he caught it before it hit the floor.

"No prob, miss. It was my fault, I shouldn't have had the box blocking my view like that."

"Well, what a goofy way to welcome you the apartments...I'm Kimbella and you are?"

"I'm Houston, Houston Burgess." And then he stuck out his index and middle fingers from the bottom of the box he was holding as a gesture for Kimbella to shake his hand. Kimbella smiled and shook those fingers gladly. Kimbella was a natural seductive person, so she grabbed those fingers with the same hollowed grip as she would if she had the opportunity to touch his manhood.

"Nice to meet you Houston and if you need someone to show you around here, I'm right underneath you in 13A."

Houston's eyes lit up when Kimbella touched him. "Well, I'm glad you offered that, cause I'm not only new to the apartment, I'm new to the area and I'd love you to lead me to a nice place for a bite to eat later."

"I'll be here all day, so stop over when you ready....how much more you have to go?"

"We're almost there...just the heavy stuff and we're good to go."

"Okay, I will be just finishing up a project, so until your stomach starts growling..." And then, Kimbella smiled at him and waked back to her apartment. He watched her walk away the best he could with that box in his eye's view before he headed back upstairs to his new apartment with it. Houston and his cousin brought the final box in at around 10:30 p.m.

"Thanks for all your help, man!" He said to James.

"No prob, just remember that you promised to fix my car next week in exchange to this...which I feel ripped off...them stairs done almost threw my back out!" He laughed, gave Houston daps and headed to his car.

Houston pulled his cell from his back pocket to check the time and noticed that it was way past 10:00. He was very hungry and quite interested in his new neighbor, Kimbella, but since it was so late he didn't want to intrude. Just as he had decided to walk up to the corner where he noticed Kimbella walking in the building with three plastic bag in her hands filled with food. Houston could clearly see that it was Chinese food.

He did a light jog towards her and asked her if she needed any help.

"Yes, I won't be able to eat all this alone. I noticed it was getting late, so I was gonna bring you and your friend something to eat."

Houston gallantly took the bags from her. "That was my cousin, James and he's gone home. Appreciate the food. Let me pay you back for the trouble."

"Oh no need. Consider it something like a welcome pie to the neighborhood."

"Well, can you at least come up and have a bite with me?"

"Well, it's pretty late, Houston and aren't you still fairly boxed up at your place?"

"True...perhaps we can eat at your place...should take only a few seconds with as hungry as I am."

She gestured with a forward tilt as she walk towards her apartment. Houston followed her all the while finally getting a good look at her backside this time. Kimbella was extremely curvy to be such a petite woman. All of 5'2" of solid muscle with firm curves in all the right places.

"Welcome to my lil abode. Place the bags over on the table while I get some plates."

"Okay." Says, Houston as he scooped the room, amazed. It was immaculate, sophisticated and somewhat sexy. It had the stench of jasmine and lavender. Her place was relaxing and very much like home in a safe, warm and comfortable kind of sense.

"Do you eat with chopsticks, Houston?"

He seemingly snaps out of the awe he felt in her apartment. "Yes, actually, I do use the chopsticks. Thanks."

Kimbella asked him to please sit and slid him a plate and began opening the firmly packed boxes of food.

"This is nice place you have here."

"It's the same design as yours, Houston. Thank you, though."

"Well, mine is far from feeling as cozy as yours. I mean, I really love how you've decorated things."

Kimbella and Houston ended up talking all night. They started with why he moved to San Francisco all the way to why Kimbella and her last boyfriend broke up. The just talked and talked as if they were old friends. She put on Friday, made popcorn and they just spent the rest of the night laughing, talking more until the wee hours of Sunday Morning. After noticing that the both fell asleep on the couch, Houston jumped up and checked his cell.

"Damn!" he grunted, still half asleep. "Kim, I'm so sorry if I overstayed my welcome last night...I really didn't mean to intrude on your kindness towards me."

Kimbella look up at him as she stretched and with a yawn in her voice said, "Houston, I loved your company. I haven't laughed that much in months...you are welcome here anytime!"

"Well, I thank you...I had a great time too...very good time!" Houston headed towards Kimbella's kitchen to clean off the table and take the trash out from that last night's Chinese food containers.

"Um, Houston, what are you doing?"

"The least I could do is help clean up before I stop invading your space."

"Houston, go finish putting together you own new apartment. Don't you still have tons to do yet? Don't worry about my place...I will clean up here, dear."

Missy Davis ordered her next latte, pondering if she wanted to allow Kimbella to be the kind of woman that gave it up quickly or the kind of woman that made a man wait. The two of them were getting along quite well and there surly was very heavy attraction. Missy decided to run through a few different options in her head as she sipped her coffee. She sat there with the shyest smirk on her face realizing that her imagination had run away with her. What had started as a clean cut meeting had somehow became a rather a steamy situation. In her head of course.

***

"It's really okay...you have so much to do. Get, scat, run along: I will clean up here."

"Well, do you have any plans for later?" Houston really didn't want leave. "I had fun with you and I'd like to have you come up later if you aren't busy."

"Give me your cell." Kimbella says with a smile. "I'll put my number in and if you think you can clear a decent walk way in your apartment...just give me a call, but dinner will be on you this time." Houston's eyes lit up at the challenge. He kissed her on the cheek and ran upstairs as fast as his long legs would carry him to make way for this (in his mind) great opportunity.

Meanwhile, Kimbella cleaned and spruced up her place and then she decided to make a quick trip to target for a few items she needed for her apartment. About three hours passed by when Kimbella got back hope from the store and notices Houston leaving the building as she was walking back in. She wondered where he was going that fast if his apartment couldn't have nearly been spruced up that fast. Kimbella didn't give it much thought. She simply carried on with enjoying and having a relaxing Sunday.

After unpacking the several bags from target, she lit a Lavender candle in the living room and a Jazmine scented one in the bathroom where she was about to draw a warm bath to soak. After her relaxing bubble bath she put on a pair of black leggings and an oversized sweater and her slipper boots. Just as she snuggled up on her sofa with a cup of hot cocoa, her cell phone rang.

"Hello."

"It's me...are you ready to come up?"

"What you mean, Houston? There is no way you finished that apartment that fast!"

"Don't say what I ain't did, Kim!" He said, laughingly.

"Well, when you want me to come up?"

"Now."

Kimbella laughed in disbelief. "Um, okay, Houston. I will be there in about thirty minutes!"

"No, now." He said firmly.

"Um, okay."

Kimbella jumped up and rushed to at least put on some mascara, lip gloss and pull her natural hair back in bun, since she had just bathed and had no thought that Houston would finish anything so quickly...especially since she's seen him leaving earlier. Kimbella walked up the one flight of stairs and knocked on the door.

Houston opened the door immediately. "Hi, Kim. So glad you came up. Come on in."

There were boxes stacked nice and neat along the hallway, but the kitchen and living room looked as if he'd been living there for months already. No decorations were up or anything, but everything was in place, table, chairs and everything was really nice so far.

"Looks nice in here, Houston! How in the world did you do this so fast and is that bbq I'm smelling?"

"I had a little bit of motivation to get it done and yes that is my famous bbq chicken in the oven."

"Wow, Houston! I am impressed!" She said as she looked over in the kitchen at the rice cooking and the rolls on the table already.

"Well, I want to make you feel as comfortable as you did for me last night." And then, Houston reached down to give her a hug. He inhaled the top of her puffy, soft natural hair. He loved the smell she gave of. She smelled like fresh cucumber and summer melons. "Damn you smell so good, Kim."

Kimbella loved that embrace. It felt so familiar, but she didn't want him to see the dream in her eyes, so she smoothly backed away and went on to say…"I had just showered when you called…demanding me to come up here." She said jokingly. "I'm a bath and body works girl and what you are smelling is the "cucumber melon" – Thanks. Looks like you'll do just fine here…I love how the place is looking."

"All your fault! You the reason I'm over here rushing around like Celie Johnson, from The Color Purple! I really enjoyed your company and I want you to see and feel that."

The look in his eyes was so endearing and honest that it made Kimbella just want to skip on whatever he was cooking and kiss him on the spot, but she'd never make moves like that with just meeting him. "I appreciate

it...smells good too...when are we eating?" She thinks
her that response hid her true feelings pretty good.

"Yep, it looks like it almost done. Just wanna thicken up
the sauce for about ten more minutes. Here taste it."
Houston dipped a wooden spoon in his special bbq
sauce and pulled Kimbella's chin in and had her taste it.
After she tasted it, he licked the rest of the sauce she
left spoon and then put the spoon in the sink. Kimbella
was extremely turned on by the way his lips and tongue
wrapped around that spoon and she was even more
turned on that he was okay with eating after her like
that.

There was getting a little harder for her hide the lustful
look in her eyes. It was as if Houston knew exactly what
he was doing. He was unwittingly be sexy as hell and
she was having a hard time controlling such a strange
desire for him. Kimbella told him the sauce was
delicious and then asked if there was anything she could
do to help out with. Houston gave her one of his aprons
and put it over her head and handed her a knife, a
bushel of romaine lettuce, and tomatoes and told her to
work on the salad while he checked on the chicken.

She looked down at the apron and read it aloud. "Kiss
the chief? How..." Just then Houston reached down to
kiss her. Houston's kiss was almost magical, so she did
the most natural thing Kimbella did since she arrived at
his apartment. She grabbed the knife he'd given her and
started chopping lettuce as fast as one of those chiefs
on those cooking channels. "Um, corny is that?' she
finally fished what she was going to say.

"Your lips taste as good as my bby sauce, Kim. Glad you asked me to kiss you." He said with a positive smirk on his face.

"Houston? She says his name with a question mark in it. "Um, how do you like your lettuce, pulled apart or neatly cut?" She changed her mind of asking her the original question that popped in her head.

"I like it plucked from the root and I like for the flower pulled inch by inch for perfect bite sized pieces. How do you like you salad?"

Kimbella's imagination went wild with the words escaping his lips. For some reason, words like pulling, plucking and flowers spoken from him seemed very erotic. "Um, yep, I like my salads like that too." She answered and dared not to even ask him how he like his tomatoes.

"Looks like the chicken is all done, Kim and when you are finished with that salad...we can eat." He said as he pulled the pan out of the oven.

Missy was pretty perplexed at how she wanted to set this scene up, but as a serious Scandal Fan, Missy thought about Olivia Pope for a moment. There is really no one on T.V. right now as sexually fluid as Kerry Washington and Shonda Rhimes always seems to keep the Olivia in the series, not only respected, but also classy and desired over and over again. As missy pondered, she seriously tried to figure out how she could go about this when a Maysa song named "Inside My Dream" and that was the moment she knew how the story would complete.

***

After pulling the pan out and placing it on the counter, Houston grabbed two plates, two wine glasses and lit a candle. He then gently pulled the apron from over Kimbella's head just as she finished the salad and walked her a few steps over to the dining room table, pulled out her chair and began serving her the bbq chicken, mixed vegetables, brown rice , a dinner role and the salad in a separate bowl on the side. And then, he fixed his own plate. Before they began eating, Houston reached across the small table and coupled Kimbella's hand.

"Do you mind if I said grace? It's very important to me to give thanks."

Kimbella was moved. "Of course not....not at all!" She actually couldn't wait to hear this man pray.

Houston bowed his head and she did the same and their hands were still clutched together. "Dear heavenly Father, we t hank you not only for this food and wherewithal to obtain it, but I personally thank you for allowing me to cross paths with such an extraordinary new friend to share it with. Thank you for my new home, new beginnings and new friendship. In Jesus name, amen"

Kimbella was awe stricken and a little guilty for becoming turned on with the way he prayed. "Looks like you've created a feast here, Houston. Everything looks so good. I can't wait to dig in." The first thing she tried was that chicken he bragged on earlier. She scooped a piece with her fork and took a bite. It melted in her mouth. It was so tender with a perfect burst of flavors all at once in her mouth. "Mmmm, OMG, Houston...this is so delicious!"

"Why thank you." He says with an assured smile.

"This, my friend, needs to be in a restaurant! My mouth is so happy right now."

"Glad you like it...I love cooking and with a reaction like that, maybe that's part of the reason why. Wout you like some wine?"

"Yes, indeed."

Houston ran to get the bottle of red wine from the fridge. "Hope you like it; it's the best thing they had in the nearest market." He poured her a sample of 2012 Theopolis Vineyards Petite Sirah in the delicate wine glass. She tasted it. "Oh my, this is delicious too. A nice burst on berries on the palate; this one is."

"Yes, I did a lil research on what were the best wines to accommodate certain meats and Theopolis Vineyards outside of California came up and when I saw it in the market; I picked it up right away. Kind of pricy, but it's all worth it if you like it." Since Kimbella seemed to like the taste, Houston poured her a full glass.

Kimbella took another sip of the wine as he poured himself a glass and asked him, "Houston, why are you dining all this for me? The meal, the rush to clean the place, the serving me and what was that kiss for?"

"All this, because I want you to know that I really like you. Besides, you did the same for me. You invited me, a perfect stranger, into your home. You entertained and fed me. How could I not want to do this for you, Kim? And the kiss, well, that was because you wanted it."

Kimbella was rather speechless, but classic held her cool. "What you mean, I wanted you to kiss me?"

Houston laughed. "I figured that would catch your attention. I see how you are looking at me, girl. You tryna act nonchalant, but I know you are feeling me...KIM!" He leaned down slowly and kissed her again. "See," he whispered, "You didn't even hesitate or push me away. You like that as much as I like you."

Kim, looking a little confused says, "Well..."

"Well, what Kim?" Houston kissed her again.

Kimbella just sat there not knowing what to say because pretty much every word he said was true. She felt like she knew this man all her life and they'd just met. She couldn't shake the feeling on familiarity with him and surely couldn't shake the attraction she had towards him. Not only because he was fin as hell, but his manhood, mannerism, the way he spoke and carried himself was very appealing. He reminds me of everything I ever desired and the way he took it upon himself to call me 'Kim' just makes me melt. Kimbella thinks to herself. 'For once in my life, I want to not play it safe, not be the well trained church girl and not worry about making the wrong decision.'

Kimbella pulled him by his pocket of his shirt. "Come here, Houston!" Suddenly an indescribable feeling overcame her as she realized a kiss was inevitable. All doubt disappeared and desire took over. She had been ignoring shortening of her breath each time he kissed her before, but no more was she not going to respond outwardly and emotionally to him. Soft at first, even uncertain, but she found the courage to return what he had been giving her since the moment they met, which was acknowledgement.

Her eyes showed a moment of hesitation, then lust gave in and her lips rushed forward. He met them with his own, slowly slipping his tongue through full lips. Kimbella could taste the berry wine on his tongue as it slowly circulated around her mouth. Houston pulled back from her lips for a moment, as though he considering something.

"Kim..." He muttered, and smiled sexily at her, pulling her closer to him. "I don't want you to think that this was all a set up. I don't want you to think that I'm one of those hit it and quit it kind of men." He pushed her chin upwards, now they were nose to nose. She could feel his warm breath on him. Her thoughts were interrupted as his lips latched onto hers again. They were so soft and gentle, and she felt everything melt. Her very meaning, her very existence, was pointless. Up until now. Abruptly, he pulled away again and just looked deep into her eyes.

"Houston," she pouted, "please don't stop. I liked that."

He smiled, his sweet, handsome smile. "I know you do."

Houston's smooth hands groped her butt and he gave her a reassuring embrace. And then he kissed her forehead. Although he approached the situation slowly (because he really didn't want her to feel like things were moving too fast) he certainly didn't want to stop. He was extremely attracted to her body and she smelled so that that he took a moment to just breathe her in.

Kimbella just decided for once to go with the flow. The room around them disappeared as well as everything around them....just him and her in his quant undone apartment. The feeling of 'right now' would leave. This feeling of 'now or never' was as vibrant as lights flashing on a dark road.

Kimbella didn't know what to expect, but she was ready for his touch. To this point, Houston was nothing less than intoxicating. Her body tried to gage where he might touch her or what he'd do after that forehead kiss, but no matter what she was ready for whatever. The first thing he did was ran his fingers through her natural, chestnut colored hair, slipping the bun loose. Her corkscrew tress fell swiftly to her shoulders as his breath gently grazed against her neck.

With him, she was more relaxed than she ever allowed herself to be with anyone. Her body had somehow allowed her to become consumed in the experience of 'him' and to only focus on the feel of his breath and lips on her neck and his tongue on her neck, now tracing a line down towards her shoulder, and across her collar bone. His tongue traced lower across her skin until reaching down, between her breasts. His breathing got faster, the closer he got as soft, warm breath tickled her skin. Houston pulled Kimbella's shirt over her arms and she perfectly let him. Her cleavage was exposed from the top of her Victoria Secret bra that he couldn't hesitate kissing. His fingers grazed across her nipples through the bra and she let out a light moan. Houston looked at her and said, "You are so beautiful, Kim." He allowed himself just a moment take in all that cleavage before returning to the dress unbuttoning process.

He unbuttoned her bra and slid it from her shoulders. His figures gave Kimbella a seductive chill all over her body. She gently laid back on the sofa and Houston's didn't hesitate to trace his tongue from her belly button and circling it, sending deep pangs of lust shooting between her legs. His tongue stopped at the top of her tights only to finish undressing me. Lying fully naked on his sofa, he is absorbing her body with his eyes in anticipation of all the things he wanted to do with it. Desire was all over his lips and his lips were all over her as if he wanted to do everything at once. Kimbella had never experience a man with such evident desire in his eyes.

"You are so sex," Houston said in a raspy whisper. Her legs started to open, ready to welcome him home, her pussy so wet and ready. His fingers moved to the insides of her thighs as he crawled up between them. She moaned and squirmed anxiously on the sofa, so aroused by the way slowly fondled me. His fingers were so close to Kimbella's wet pussy that she ached for him to touch her there.

Suddenly he kissed her naval downward until he reached the spot she yearned him to touch, kiss and fill. She felt his breath seconds before his tongue touched her sweet spot, so softly it was almost agony it was such pure pleasure. Her clit pulsed under the wetness of his tongue and she cried out with sheer delight as he began working his tongue in small circles. Her hands grabbed the back of his head as she arched her back and opened her legs wider, gyrating beneath his mouth. Kimbella was elevated to a state of pure bliss, as if having an out of body experience.

His tongue moved lower, licking the moist lips, lapping up her juices, and every time he licked she was desperate to feel him slip his tongue deep inside of her. She pulled slightly on the back of his head, pulling him closer and then he did it and he pushed his tongue deep into her. She almost melted as his tongue flicking in and out, in and out. Seconds later his thumb found her clit and began stroking it softly, in time with his tongues movements. She gasped, moaned and thrust her pelvis backwards and forwards onto his face with the rhythm of his movements. There was nothing but this moment, the feeling and the pure perfect pleasure of him pleasing her beyond measure.

Houston guided her hand to his throbbing, hard, manhood. She wrapped her fingers around him eagerly, pulling him off firmly in time with his tongue fucking her. In Kimbella's, the sensation she was feeling was from a different world and she wanted to experience it fully. She came all over his face rapidly. Houston stood up beside her and took his shirt off, his jeans pulled down around his thighs as he bent over to kiss her. She opened her mouth to taste herself on his lips as he rubbed her swollen clit.

She sat up on the sofa with his dick facing her and licked the swollen head, teasing him with her tongue, as her hand continued to stroke the shaft firmly. His cock filled her mouth as she sucked him off. Her pussy grew hotter and even wetter with every stroke, in and out. Houston was thick and long. She heard him groan deeply, and felt the head of his erect penis dripping as she lapped and licked it all. She sucked hard as she worked her mouth up and down, cupping his heavy testicles with her hand.

There was never a chance of him lasting much longer, but she wanted to taste everything he had to offer, so she licked in a circular motion at the head of his cock with each in and out motion. Hearing Houston's groans as she pleasured him caused her pussy to pulsate. She gently squeezed his balls again whilst sucking down hard. He thrust his pelvis up against her and she felt his cum shooting into the back of her mouth. And, with unhesitant pleasure she received it all.

Houston looks at Kimbella and says, "Next time dinner is at your place!"

Missy Davis sat there in the coffee shop noticing that the place was closing. She had no idea so much time had passed by. Missy began packing her things to leave, totally overwhelmed that she allowed characters to have such lucid sex with having just met. She thought to herself that these are people that she'd not quickly forget about.

***

About Katrina Gurl

Katrina Gurl is a Relationship Coach by day in Bellingham, Washington and an erotic writer by night.

In 2009, Katrina's dream came true when she became a published author of The Balcony View Revisited and thanks to her wonderful readers; she has become even more in love and dedicated to writing.

She loves hot white mocha's as she writes, hates writing one story at a time and is afraid of cornfields (yes, cornfields) and people that don't blink their eyes in the proper amount of increments...which(on average) is approximately once every five seconds. She went to college for a business and ended up a writer with degree in mathematics. So rest assured her characters will always have a great budget and balanced checkbook.

Katrina wants the romantic, seductive and alluring books to be as the first, filled with erotic stories and twists of fate.

Her life took a turn of events when she first published The Balcony View Revisited. As soon as Katrina hit her mid-thirties, she had a desire to write love stories that readers would fall in love with...realistic love stories!

She is more than ready to complete her next book of short stories.

Languid Effect
by Emmanuel Brown

You've been ceaseless since the beginning of our time

That first glimpse of allurement you shared, seemed to

be sublime

Unsurement followed, my resistance hollowed

To a shell of unprotection, my logic was soon swallowed

I couldn't restrain the anxious thoughts you embedded
in my soul

In every empty fold, and unchartered parts of me, truth
be told

You said "man behold", without uttering a word

My stuttering slurred, ummahhmm is what was

heard But I caught your attention, not to mention - a

special part of you

But I was so blinded that I couldn't see the start of you I

didn't even know that you knew that I existed

I didn't take any shots because I was sure that they'd

be misses

Boldly you blew kisses, when I began to speak in

English Then you told me that I acted really Kingish

I became fiendish, caught up in your rapture

Visiting day and night, allowing you to capture

Every gram of me, while I consumed the whole you

While the man in me realized that I had stole you

No need to control you because your strength was a
strong suit

But to hold you, we both knew was really the wrong suit

We had borrowed time and space from places
that weren't ours

But we rolled around in flowers, testing the depths of
our powers

We reached climactic peaks far beyond the reach
of Earth

You surrounded my girth, like no other, for what it's
worth

Your forbidden fruit was more mine than it was yours

I even smelled your steamy trails escaping from
my pores

You're so erotically tranquil, the storm before my
calms
I'd be beyond foolish to let you slip from my palms

You love my confidence, fact is, I'm that man that
you can count

My word, mind, body and soul is yours; always in a
whole amount

I just had a mushy moment, now let get myself in check

I truly hope, for my sake, that we share this
languid effect

About Emmanuel Brown

Emmanuel Brown is a father, program administrator, webmaster, the founder of Seeing Growth and Editorial Director of Label Me Royalty. Emmanuel promotes the idea of Seeing Growth in all aspects of life through the use of positive self-confidence. That is just one statement that describes who Emmanuel Brown is.

He has parlayed a disadvantaged upbringing, in one of Chicago's most impoverished and violent areas, into a motivating attribute of daily routines that consist of merging the positive influences of many people into an assortment of opportunities and inspiration for everyone that wants to receive and contribute to the concept of community building.

Emmanuel Brown believes that anyone can be reached if they are reached for by the right person, and that the people who seem unreachable have not been reached because their visions have been blocked by self-created boundaries. Emmanuel Brown has no intentions of slowing down and plans to share his visions long after he is gone.